I Ride a Ten Speed
(actually a one speed)...
and Other Funny Little Stories
About Dating

www.mcnallyrobinson.com/selfpublishing

First Edition
978-1-77280-236-8

I Ride a Ten Speed (actually a one speed)… and Other Funny Little Stories About Dating

TENNESSEE JACKSON

Dedication

I dedicate this book to my dear friend Tracy, who has taught me how to embrace life, be positive and approach each dating experience with optimism and excitement. She should have written a book about her predictions about dating. Each and every one was true. Cheers Tracy! I love you like crazy. And I will never forget the way you look at every dating challenge and opportunity, at the very least, as great conversation, dinner or a coffee. You got that right girlfriend, so thank you.

Contents

I Ride a Ten Speed
and
How It All Began

To be honest, I never dreamed I would be able to use all of my experiences personally to write this book. I never dreamed that I would have enough crazy stories to fill up an actual book, nor did I dream that I would meet the types of people that I did. I also didn't realize that I was meant to be single, and to meet all of the people that I did on my journey, or how significant they would all be in contributing to my story. Here is where it all began.

I had gone through a messy break-up. I know we all say that, but I was devastated and pessimistic really, as well as very doubtful that I could go on without him, or that I would survive. I did, however, know that I had to keep going and that I had to survive. I had heard all of the hype about online dating, about Plenty of Fish, about Match.com, and had seen so many countless commercials about eHarmony, that I almost felt a bit nauseated.

I remember sitting down at the computer, to figure out how to get started, while at my mom's place. I sat down at the desk, opened up Match.com, and this is where it all began. As I perused so many really crazy profiles, funny faces, and sometimes scary people, I found a very handsome young man who I thought could be the one. With my fingers as my search engine, and my heart in my hand, I decided to reach out and talk to him.

I sent him a little message, after taking several minutes to try to figure out how to do just that – literally send him a message. After all, I knew how to use a cell phone and could text, so how much harder could this be, I thought? As I pressed send and the message travelled through space to get to him, I sat patiently in my chair waiting for my Prince Charming to stand up and come to life. He would tell me how wonderful I was, sweep me off of my feet, and this is how we would begin our story.

Instead, his response was a bit silly. I remember giggling quietly to myself in embarrassment, and hiding the screen when my mom walked into the room. After all, online dating and talking with a stranger on the computer, was a bit creepy as well as a bit weird. I felt guilty flirting with the poor guy, and felt almost sympathetic to the thought that he may have felt guilty about having to respond to my message.

He asked my name, what I did for a living, where I lived, and what I was up to. I thought the questions were kind and thoughtful, so I responded. I continued and asked his marital status and what he did for a living. He quickly responded that he was home alone and that he and his "ex-wife" were separated, but that they continued to live in the same house. "Hmmmmm", I thought to myself, "that is a bit funny". But since he was honest, I felt I should give him the time of day just for his token of honesty. As he began to tell me more about their situation, and how he was technically single and available, I had a bit of a tense gut and you know that kind of "you know this isn't right don't you, silly girl?" feeling, but I continued to talk.

He asked what I did for fun. I told him I liked being outdoors, that I loved my family, and that I loved to ride my bike. I really don't ride my bike very often, but it made me giggle so it was worth it for me to say something odd. I remember my girlfriends and I joking about riding a ten speed when we were kids, and how "uncool" that would be nowadays, so I thought I have nothing to lose. He then asked what kind of bike I had and I told him I had a ten speed, laughing hysterically to myself, while my Mom stood laughing herself, watching the messages light up the screen. After all, some people don't even know what a ten speed is. He quickly responded and said, "well ride that ten speed on over to my place". He said he was home alone and needed some company to help with his lonely little soul. I laughed hysterically and chose not to respond.

Needless to say, I don't ride a ten speed, nor do I own one. I have learned that some guys will say all the right things to get a ticket into your life. They don't care if you ride a ten speed, some probably don't even care if you have legs. They will tell you whatever they need to in order to go along for the ride.

And so as it is, this is where it all began. I got on my ten speed and prepared myself for the ride of my life, this journey we call dating.

Tennessee

I don't really know where my name came from. Tennessee. It was sweet and sexy, but yet a bit mysterious. Somehow I thought it sounded like a name that would make me famous and end me up in Nashville, but it didn't.

I guess it was a combination of a lot of things. The name Tennessee was every bit country, a whole lot of Nashville, and a touch of Michael Jackson, all in one word. I guess it's about who I am. I am a single woman in my forties, who has been dating and single for several years since my break-up. I love so many things about life. The simple things. the little things. Giggling, rain drops, laughter, family, friends, the great outdoors. Life for me is all about what makes me tick and the things that bring me joy.

And yes of course, there's a little bit of Johnny Cash in me. He was strong and sexy. He was beautiful, and he made Nashville a legend. Tennessee is my name. I love men. I love men in black. And I love Johnny Cash.

The rollercoaster ride I have been on for the last six years has been wild and crazy, as well as faster than I imagined. It's been scarey and gut-wrenching, and at the same time, the time of my life. No regrets, I always say, and I guess I really mean that. My name is Tennessee. Hop into the passenger seat. We're going for a ride.

500 Miles to Tennessee

My very dear friend once told me that I need to find a man who would drive five hours, just to see me for one. I never understood that, perhaps because I never had anyone put me on a pedestal like that, or perhaps because I never expected that of anyone.

I remember looking at my friend and her husband, very dearly, one day. He had driven countless miles to see her when they first began dating, and they are now one of the few genuinely happy couples that I know. I admire them both and I admire him for being a good man, a wonderful care provider, and a wonderful friend to me.

I guess in some ways I never thought I deserved a man who would drive 500 miles, or five hours, just to see me. But as time has passed, and I have met many men who I know would never had done this for me, I really hoped that someday God would send me someone who would put me on that pedestal, and do anything just to see me.

Well the moment came true. I remember asking so many times for someone to bring a good man into my world. I tried very hard not to lose hope that one day he would walk right into my life and fit exactly where he is supposed to be. I met him online. He was beautiful and thoughtful, as I had hoped in my mind. He showed his heart in every message, with respect and dignity and the kinds of qualities I always hoped I would find in a man.

He lived in another part of the world. He lived so far from me that I figured we would write forever and we would never get to meet. I remember my last prayer that this good man would find me and walk into my life like he was supposed to. I remember the email. "I'm heading your way," he said, and the pit in my stomach grew large. I didn't expect it. I didn't believe it would happen. And most of all I didn't think he would follow through. I knew if I was the guy considering spending hours on the road in order to get to see me, that I was worth it, but he had no way of knowing just that.

He did just that. He hopped in his truck and drove over 500 miles to see me. He put on his stereo, and his foot on the gas, and didn't hesitate to get here. And to tell you the truth, I don't think I can recall a moment where I felt luckier in my dating life. I still didn't believe he would get here, that he would step out in front of me and bless my world for the very first time, and our very first real-life introduction, but he did.

I now know that feeling of meeting a man who is willing to drive as long as it takes to see you, just because he wants to. He thinks you're worth it, and I know that I am, but after many failed dating experiences, and men who did not make me a priority, I didn't think it would happen. The moment was amazing, and my heart grew like a flower the first day it gets sunshine on that very first day of spring.

I remember him leaving. I had no idea if I would ever see him again, as I knew the distance would be a challenge for both of us. I knew if he felt even a piece of the butterflies and attraction and gratefulness that I did, that he would make it back. He kissed me goodbye and gave me a hug that I will never forget. I told him we didn't need to say goodbye, instead that we would see each other soon, and I knew in my heart that we would.

So my friend, never cut yourself short. I think we are our own worst critics. Women accept less than we know we are worth, and pray that a man is going to give us more than that. I guess we need to be more adept at knowing what we want, and be more patient while we wait for it.

Don't ever forget that you're worth it. No matter what the situation, a man needs to deserve you. He should be willing to make the effort, and make some sacrifices in order to get a place in your heart. After all, like my dear friend tells me, a good man will drive five hours just to see you for one. Thank you baby, for making the effort of driving 500 miles to Tennessee. Xo.

Sorry

I cannot count how many times I have prayed that one day I would run into the man that broke my heart and he would tell me, after all that time had passed, that he was sorry. He would prove to me that he was, and would admit that he made a mistake and was coming back to get me.

I guess that isn't reality. It just doesn't happen that way. But I guess the point of that is that if it wasn't meant to be, the man is not supposed to come back. He is not supposed to apologize, nor is he in any position to admit that he was wrong, or that he made a mistake. But I have enjoyed the moment of a man that broke my heart attempting to walk back into my life, on one of those nights that I felt like I was on top of the world, and nothing could stop me, or make me think for a second about stepping back into those shoes.

The day finally arrived. He walked into the room. I had thought about him countless times since he broke my heart, and ended us in a text message. I hated him for a very long time, angry at the cold nature of how he was ending our relationship in a text.

I felt good that night. I think I looked amazing. I had taken good care of myself since we had dated, and I was proud of myself and who I had become. I scanned the room, taking full note of his location, and made every effort to pretend I did not see him.

As I focused on everything else in the room, in order to avoid putting any focus on him, I felt a tap on my shoulder. As I turned around, my heart skipped a beat. It was him. He was gorgeous and smelled amazing, just like those days when we were seeing each other. I did feel some glory in his words. He squirmed with each and every one of them, but I knew he had a story that he wanted to share. I acted calm and friendly, anxious to hear what he had to tell me.

He told me he had deleted my number, and that he missed me ever since that day, and that a lot had happened since then. He reminisced about how we "clicked", and how he found it amazing, and how he had only realized it in retrospect. He touched my hair and leaned closer, and all over again, I was back in the moment, my heart was open, desperate to let him in and love me again.

He quickly wanted to start where we left off. As much as I wanted to do that, I was scared, reluctant, and afraid that letting my brakes up would end up opening my heart to disaster, only to have my heart broken again. I took him outside and told him what I was thinking. I told him he broke my heart, that he ended us in a text. He sighed, almost to say that he did not realize what he had done, and reached out to give me a hug. I let my guard down and let him in again. He held me and told me he was sorry. In some weird kind of way it helped to heal my broken heart.

As much as we want to hold a grudge when someone hurts us or breaks our hearts, as human beings we want to love and we want to find peace. Holding a grudge against someone for the rest of our lifetime does nothing but hurt us. We have to continue to believe that people are good, that they want to be good, and that they have no real intention or purpose of hurting us.

We have to let go of the pain, let go of the anger, in order to heal and fully move on to someone else. We just can't take that damage with us. Kind words, and a man who can think about what he has done go a long way. I am sorry. Three funny little words that can open a whole new world for us and help us to heal and move on. Thank you mister, I accept your apology. I am at peace.

Straight Up

Do you ever get defensive when one of your dearest friends tells you the honest truth or their honest opinion about dating? Do you cringe when they tell you what your heart knows is true, but get angry and sometimes refuse to believe what they tell you? Well I have, and I regret it. I always say that I thrive on people being honest with me, yet I am a hypocrite when some of my very best friends tell me the truth.

I believe fully that one of the best pieces of advice I have received about dating was from a man. I can count on both hands the amount of men that I have dated who did not tell me the truth, and who told me everything they could other than that, to lead me to believe they were on the same page as I was.

It wasn't long ago that I ran into a man that I had only known for a short time. He asked how I was, attempted to rekindle what we had back then, and thought for certain that we could just carry off from where we left off. He didn't seem surprised when I told him we couldn't. Men aren't stupid, but they sometimes get away with whatever they think that they can, or whatever we let them.

When I explained the reason behind why we could not start where we had left off a few years ago, in that I was seeing someone else, he gave me the best minute of advice I could ask for. I told him that I was seeing someone, that I had seen a few people since we had met, and that I never really knew how to read men or their intentions.

Simply, he told me this. He said if a man is interested in you and knows where you stand in his life, he will tell you. If he doesn't know, he isn't going to be able to tell you. If you ask him what you are, and what you mean to him, and ask him to put a label on it and he can't, it's simply because he doesn't want to. He doesn't know what you are, a girlfriend, a booty-call, or someone convenient, and doesn't tell you because he doesn't know. If he knows that you are his girlfriend, his partner, his lover, his friend, or someone that he hopes to see in his life in his future, you will know it because he will make sure that you know.

It's simple. When you ask a man what is going on and he panics, it's because he doesn't know or doesn't care. If he refuses to talk about his feelings or how he feels about you, perhaps it's because he doesn't feel anything. With the exception of a few good men who have a hard time talking about their feelings, the majority of men don't tell you how they feel about you because they don't feel anything.

I once dated a man for two years. I asked several times throughout our "relationship" what we were, and he said nothing. He sat silent, completely emotionless about what I had just asked him. I asked and I asked, begging for him to tell me how important I was, and he would smile and say nothing. At the end of us dating, and my pressuring him so much for a label that he called it quits, I was grateful that he did. He didn't want to label us because I wasn't important. He wasn't on the same page, didn't feel the same way, and didn't want the same things I did. I am grateful for the conversation that day, as I would still be being dragged along, absolutely clueless about the fact I meant next to nothing to him.

Thank you to the man who opened my eyes to a reality that I often don't see. Sometimes it's hard to hear other people tell you what you yourself aren't willing to see, but it's so important to let it absorb and see the clarity in it. Men who love you and want to be with you will let you know it. Men who see you as a life partner will introduce you to their loved ones, their children, their parents, their friends. They won't hide you in the closet as a dirty little secret. They will be proud of you. They will be so excited to tell the world about you that they can hardly conceal it. It's all about honesty. Straight up, blunt, but wonderful honesty, you are truly a gift.

No Regrets

I really can say that I have no regrets about every man I have ever dated or invested in. Each and every one has taught me something about what I love, what I hate, and what I need to have, in order to feel valued and loved.

The man who broke my heart and cheated on me taught me about being faithful, being honest, and how important it is to not fall head over heels in love with someone before you really know who they are. Take your time, enjoy the moment, and try not to take for granted the things that your heart knows you don't want.

The man who was kinky and twisted will teach you what you like or don't like. When he asks to sleep with your friends, you can quickly identify his motive and move on. You can look for another man, who will be content with having you in his life, without a need to sleep with your friends.

The man who denied being in a relationship with you will teach you that you need to ask men the tough questions early on in the relationship. You need to ask what they are looking for, how they see dating fitting into their life, and what their long term dating plans are. If they squirm and run, well frankly perhaps you should too.

The man who said he wasn't wanting to be with you because you "didn't have your shit together", is the one who taught you to keep searching for a good man. He gave you the glory you needed when you found out his vanity ended him up in divorce number two, because he couldn't find anyone who fit his mould. He wanted the white picket fence and complete perfection. He now sits in his living room, looking out the window alone.

I guess it's all about how we go into anything. We can go into a relationship pessimistic or bitter, or we can go into it light-heartedly, asking all the tough questions that we need to ask up front. We can dive head first into a relationship with anyone who pays attention to us, or we can take it slow and know that a good man who wants to have you in his life will not be in a hurry.

Take your time. Slow down and remember to breathe. Enjoy the moment. Experience the joy. And when the crazies enter your life, keep your butt near the door so you can exit as quickly as possible. Remember, no regrets. Enjoy each and every lesson that a man can teach you. But don't be taken for granted or get blind-sided. Advocate for you. You are the only one who can do that.

Take It Off

While shopping today with my very dear friend and begging her to come into this shop with me, we came across a great sale. Most things in the store were marked down to a dollar, even bras and panties.

What I realized today, for the 100th time, and for the ninety- nine other times that I didn't, is that men don't care about underwear, instead they only care about taking it off. As I shared my thoughts about this with my boyfriend at the time, he shared with me men's real thoughts.

Men don't care about underwear. They prefer when you don't even have any on. Personally, I need a part-time job, and a separate bank account, for the amount of money I spend on underwear. I can't recall how many times I have gotten excited in the lingerie section, picking out the sexiest panties or bra, or even a set, so excited that I couldn't wait to get home and put it on.

I also can't believe or recall how many times I have put on the damn sexy outfit and spent the night with my boyfriend, only to realize later that he didn't even look at it. He didn't care. He didn't notice it. He didn't get excited.

So ladies, stop spending all that crazy money on underwear for a man. Remember you don't need a man to feel sexy. Buy the crazy underwear for you. Put it on under your work clothes and feel like a million bucks. No one else will figure out your secret to looking so fabulous, and for giving off a vibe that is so sexy and positive, others won't help but notice.

Sexy is about you. Sexy is about loving who you are, not what you look like. Sexy is how you feel about yourself, and how it is portrayed to the man you love. If you love who you are, he will notice. He will love to be with you just the way you are, regardless of your underwear. Sexy is great. Sexy is wonderful, but it all begins with loving who we are first.

You'll Think of Me

Its funny. I bought a new car on the weekend and tonight I really wanted to show it to you. It's been two years and I still think of you. Perhaps it's the odd video you send me on facebook, just to make sure you pop into my life randomly, every once in a while.

Brad was the kind of guy you loved to love, or loved to hate. He had a smile and a charm that would win you over, or else make you instantly hate him. He had a body of an athlete and a butt made of lead, all which made him even harder to walk away from when it ended.

I met Brad through friends. Although he was eight years younger than I was, I fell for him harder than I ever fell for anyone. I met him Halloween night with some buddies, having no idea that I was going to meet the man I would fall in love with, nor did I know ahead of time that I needed to get myself all done up.

As we sat together across the table, my heart was ticking like a giant clock, hoping that he would feel that same click that I did. The night progressed and before we knew it we were texting each other across the table, while our friends knew nothing. We hit it off that night and that's where our story began.

Brad and I dated for several years. I loved him from the minute he was introduced to me, and that only grew each and every time I spent time with him. He was sweet and charming, taught me about kindness and love, and always took time to make sure I was okay.

As time progressed, my heart grew bigger and more in love with him. I never doubted that he loved me back and that he was the one, until one day I felt a bit weird about things. I thought to myself I had never asked him what we were, and if we were an item, yet I had never really panicked that I had to. I asked him what was going on, I guess in a sense pressuring him to put a label on us, and in return he said nothing. The silence killed me. I asked him to talk to me and he said just that – nothing. So I got him in my car and drove him around, pretending we were going to go shopping.

I pulled into a parking lot at the mall. I put the car in park and asked him what was going on. I told him we were not going shopping, that we needed to talk, and the silence in the car at that moment could have cut paper.

As I asked the dreaded question, I knew in my heart that the answer was not one that I wanted to hear. He told me he didn't want a relationship, that he never thought we were in one, and that he wasn't the relationship kind. I cried like a baby. I cried most of that day, and spent months pining over my loss. I loved him more than I had ever loved anyone, and could not believe how he chose to break my heart. After all, how could he not feel what I felt? How could he pretend that he did?

I cried every weekend, for many months, until one day my body couldn't take the heartbreak and told me to get up, put my big girl panties on, to be strong, and to move on.

Perhaps Brad was bittersweet. He taught me things that I needed to know. He taught me things about what I was missing – cuddles, kindness, thoughtfulness, hugs. He taught me what it felt like to be silly and giggle, and to hold hands during a movie. Before him, I had forgotten what those things felt like, and he reminded what they were and how much I had missed them.

Brad, I thank you for teaching me all kinds of things, and I guess I forgive you for breaking my heart. You weren't feeling what I felt, and I am glad that you were honest enough to tell me that. I miss you sometimes. Today I wanted to show you my car, for whatever reason that was, and I even drove by your house. I saw two cars in front, knowing full well you have probably found it very easy to find someone else to love you. I have moved on but I still think of you. And every time I get a video or an email from you on Facebook, I know you still think of me. I knew you would look back and think we had a good thing, whether or not that was enough to bring you back to me. And to be honest, I know you haven't forgotten me. I was good to you, kind and caring, and I loved you more than anything. You will think of me again. I know you will.

Bacon, Bikinis and Another Man's Wife

I think when it comes down to it, men and women really are different. We think different. We act different. Our priorities are different. I know myself that I often look at all of my guy friends, and the men who I have dated, and go "wtf", what in the world makes us think that we are meant to be together?

At a conference one week at work, the girls and I sat around and compared notes about men, those that we dated, those that we married, those that we dreamt about, and those that we worked with. We thought about it long and hard and had so many laughs, I can still feel my stomach hurting when I think back to our conversation.

We thought about what makes guys tick. What do they think about when they like us, and what do they think about while we spend days thinking about all the ooey-gooey things that they probably don't spend a single second thinking about.

Women wear their hearts on their sleeves. Men, in my opinion, don't. I think men care and men have feelings, of course they do, but when women spend hours and days, even weeks, reminiscing about a moment, a feeling, a hug, a kiss, or something that made us go "aww", I often wonder if men spend a single second thinking back, or dwelling on that exact moment like we do. I don't think they do.

I remember, as an example, of a time when I layed in bed with my partner. We hugged and cuddled for hours, and laughed about things like we were little kids, purely in a moment of joy that I cannot explain. We clicked like I never really had clicked with anyone, and I felt like the world had stopped in that very moment while we were together.

I remember for weeks thinking back to that moment when we were just laying there, the door closed to the rest of the world, thinking I was the luckiest girl in the world. I remember lighting up with a smile on my face, each and every time I thought about that moment, how he touched me, how he made me laugh, how he kissed me like I meant everything. And then I wonder, did he spend a single minute looking back at that moment like I did? Then I realized, no, he probably didn't.

I think men have good hearts and they think about things. But they don't dwell on them, over-inflate them, or make a moment bigger than it was. They enjoy the moment. They feel the passion. They enjoy the hugs and cuddles of the moment, but they move on. They continue with their day. They don't keep looking back at that very moment, and make it last forever, like we do.

Then we talked about what we think makes men tick? Do they race home after work thinking about what they are going to eat? Do they race home on Friday, thinking about the bacon they are going to make for breakfast Saturday morning, or do they instead get really excited about the fact they are going to see us tonight, and nothing else matters?

Truth is, they just take life as it comes. They love women. They love breasts. They love a challenge. And they love being cared for. But truthfully, I don't think they think about stuff like we do. They like us. They love us. They enjoy us. But they truly don't get all gushy when they think about us, like we do when we think about them.

They love bacon. They love trucks. They love taking pictures of themselves, proudly holding a dead fish or a deer's head when they conquer that part of being a man. They love fast cars. They love football. They love hockey. They love hanging out with the guys. They like to be one of the guys. They love women's bodies. They drool over them. They compare them. They dream about them. But again, they generally don't obsess about them. They enjoy the minute they have in each situation, and that's it. They live in the moment. To be honest, I am a bit envious of that. They live in a moment and move on to the next, and I guess I admire them for that.

Men love bikinis. They love naked women. They love to have a variety of naked women to look at, whether that be on a dating site, in real life, or in a dirty magazine. Regardless, they like to have a pocket full of women and experiences to think about and look back at, or forward to. They like to sit and stare at women on the beach, or at the hot waitress in the pub who is nice to them. They are confident that each one of them has a genuine interest in them beyond a tip and nice conversation.

Men love the beauty of another man's wife. They love women in power, especially those in the media. The ones who are beautiful and untouchable, taken, or just out there hanging in the midst of reality, but those that are truly not available to anyone. They like to imagine what life would be like with those women, with the glory of pretending they could have them.

I guess what we need to realize, or I need to realize, is men are not as emotional as we are. They don't dwell on words. They don't dwell on moments. They try to live in the moment, and in a sense I guess we should appreciate that. They don't break down every word that is said like we do, or break down the intent of every moment.

It's simple. We are women. We are beautiful. We are powerful. We are thinkers and feelers. We are amazing. Men, on the other hand, are not like us. They strive to be powerful, strong, put-together, amazing. And often they are just that. They enjoy moments, not memories, as much as we do. They have big hearts and sometimes wear them on their sleeves, but I think overall they are more practical and sensible than we are.

So ladies, let's try to remember our differences, and learn to appreciate them. I know I personally do enough thinking for both sexes, so I don't need to pressure anyone to think more than I already do. Enjoy the moment with your partner. Enjoy that they live less restrictively than we do, and hope that some of that free spirit rubs off on us. I know I could use a little less worry, a little less days of over-thinking everything, and a moment to just enjoy a moment for what it is.

And remember, men find joy in women, period. They love us. They cherish us. They want us to be happy. If they don't want those things for you, then act like they do, and move on. Find someone who loves you like they love bacon, bikinis and another man's wife.

On Your Mark, Get Set, Go!

If you had one minute to list five things you love about your partner, could you do it? If you can't clearly think of five things that you love about the person you are with, within a one minute period, then maybe you need to think about that. Give it some thought. Why are you with them? Do they bring you joy, do you bring them joy, do they make your heart go pitter-patter?

I have given this much thought, and I fully believe that it is so important to know if the person you are with is right for you. Does he make you giggle, does he know that you're ticklish, does he know your middle name and the color of your eyes, does he make you kick your feet when you talk to him, and does he bring you joy? Does he make you smile when you are sitting in a crowded room full of people?

If he lights that fire in you and he knows your beauty and who you really are, hang onto him. Love him. Appreciate him. Accept his quirks. Accept that he snores. Wear earplugs if you have to. Hug him and kiss him every chance you get, and thank him for being a gift in your life. Tell him what he means to you and mean it. I think we often take things for granted and forget to tell our loved ones how much they mean to us. Think about how you feel when someone says how much they love you, be that a friend or a loved one, or when you feel like a gift in someone's world.

We all need to be wanted, to be appreciated, to be loved. Every moment that we invest in another person, when they are right for us, will bring us good results. A man who is treasured for who he is, without any pressure to change, will appreciate us in return. A good man who loves you will appreciate your love for him. Admire him. Be proud of him. And when you're in a crowded room standing beside him, be grateful for the moment and the gift of his blessing in your life.

I know as a woman, and an individual, I feel the joy of being appreciated and loved. I love a man who is proud of me, the man who walks beside me, and not in front of me. I love a man who thanks me for dinner, and holds my hand with pride when we walk down the street. I really believe that we have to invest in our partner and cherish them the way we want them to cherish us.

Good luck ladies. On your mark, get set, go! Go find him. And when you do, tell him he is beautiful and thank him for his gifts. Teach him all of your little secrets, tell him that you're ticklish, and remember to love him if he's worth it. Loving him will work a hundred- fold in return. He will race home to see you at the end of the day, and he will want to spend as many moments in the day with you.

Deal Breaker

We all know the story. You date this wonderful man. You dream about him every night, and fantasize how he will fit into your future, and the joy and glory that he will bring you. You think he's the one. He's the greatest, or so you think, and he is the best thing that has walked into your life.

He may be the best lover, he loves your family, does all the right things, has all the right moves, and then all of a sudden, out of the blue, he does something wrong. He isn't the guy you thought he was. He treats you like shit after a bad day at work, or just so happens to forget your birthday.

Let's face it girls. We have all been there. We have all lived the story. We have all loved someone throughout our lives that we thought were truly perfect. However, we all know that no one is perfect, and sometimes those rose-colored glasses are dangerous.

For me, there are many deal breakers. A deal breaker is this. It is something that I may put up with once, but only because I didn't expect ir or see it coming. It's the guy who says he wants you to be a part of his life and family, but doesn't invite you to Sunday dinner at his parents. He expects you to come over after dinner, but fails to invite you for the meal. He thinks you will be waiting for him, no matter what you have going on, to come over and be at his beck and call when he needs you.

That's a deal breaker. It's the guy who says all the right things, but forgets to roll over and wish you a happy birthday when he wakes up. He's the man who forgets to tell you you are special at a time when you need to hear it the most.

By no means am I perfect. I know none of us, including myself, are. A huge part of a healthy relationship is based on dating a person who knows first-hand what is important to you, and makes every effort to make it important to him as well.

Don't settle for less. Make him aware of what is important to you so that when he forgets it, or shows you a different side of him, that you can remind him about what matters. The first time he forgets is his fault. The second time he forgets is yours. If we don't tell them, there is no way that they will know what we want or what we need.

And finally, expect respect and I believe you will receive it. Keep your standards high, and the right man will knock down your door to find you and meet your expectations. Don't ever give up or settle for less than you know you deserve.

Wild Heart

I want a man who has a wild heart, one who says it like it is, one who isn't afraid to show his true colors, and one who has passion. His passion will make my heart beat faster, and put roses in my cheeks. He will love everything about his life, and everything in the big old world that makes his life worthy.

I want a man who will love to be tickled. I want a man who has a wild heart and feels happy and sad and angry, all at the right time, and who feels passion about something. It can be anything. A man just needs to have passion.

A wild heart will not be afraid to live, to love, to laugh, to be hurt. to take a chance, to lose, or to get a few scars on the way. He will also take a ride to places he never expected. He will love, he will feel, and he will care. His wild heart will take him places he never thought he would get to, and he will enjoy every minute of it.

A man with a wild heart will be willing to give and to love and to share. He will be afraid to let himself go and give his heart to someone, just like we are, but he will do it because he knows in the end it will be worth it.

He will take you on a wild ride. He will love you. He will cherish you. He will have your back when you need him. And he will have a white horse that he rides on, when he walks into your life and world, and leaves you breathless.

Must-Haves

I think as we get older we begin to realize what we need and search for the man who can give that to us.

I want a man who knows he is a good man. He is kind and hard working, and he is honest. He wants to share his life with me and make me a part of every piece of his life, not just portions of it. He will be so proud of me that he will look forward to every new introduction, to his parents, to his children, to his friends. He will hold your hand in public, and only have eyes for you when you are out, and he will take pride in you.

He will tickle me and hug me and want to be silly. He will take life seriously, but will also take time to enjoy it. Life goes fast, and it's so worth it for you to enjoy it. He will have my back. He will stick up for me, as us old school girls would call it, and do what he has to do when others try to hurt me or put me in danger. In our honor, a good man will do whatever they need to, in order to keep us safe and to protect us.

In my eyes, a good man will remember my birthday, and when he does he will make sure to acknowledge it. He will always buy me a card, even if he cannot afford anything but a card. He will write some kind of crazy message to me, about how much I mean to him, and make me feel like I am very lucky to have him in my life.

A good man won't be afraid to do hard labor and sweat, especially when it comes to me needing to move to a new home. Whether he likes it or not, he will be the first one at my door to help, and the last guy off the truck on moving day, after all of my belongings have been moved.

A good man will remember how lucky he is. He will be the first New Year's Eve greeting that I get, and the first one that he sends. A good man will be kind and loving. He will hug you when you need it, and will know when you are hurting and need him. He will hug you because you are sad, he will hug you because you need one, and he will hug you because he also needs to feel loved. He won't be afraid to care, and he won't be afraid to love you. He will show kindness and be able to show his love with a hug.

A good man will be excited to see me. He won't lick my face and jump on my leg like my dog used to, but he will get just as excited, as he waits for me to get home. He will smile when I walk through the door and will be so very excited to tell me about his day, and be willing to share his with me.

A good man will ask you how your day was. He will want to know and he won't be afraid to tell you about his. He won't fret when you swear and tell him how horrible the day was, how unfair your boss is, or how your friend pissed you off. He will listen patiently, and be there for you no matter how that day looked.

A good man will dance with me. He won't hesitate to seize the opportunity to hold me in his arms and swing me around the room, even when there's no music. He will take me to a wedding and charm my socks off on the dance floor. He will make the bride and groom stare in awe at how in love we are. He won't worry that he isn't a good dancer or tell me "I can't dance", or "I don't dance". Instead he will seize every chance he gets to dance with me. He won't need to know how, or to be good at it, but he will have the courage and be willing to try.

And finally, a good man will want to make me part of his family. I will meet his parents, his siblings, his children, and anyone else he considers to be important.

Girls, we all need a man who loves us and would do anything for us, and they are out there. They really are. If you haven't met him yet, keep looking. He's out there, you just have to find him. And when you do you will know it. He will have every single must-have that you are looking for, and will bring joy to your life, just like you thought he would.

Why Didn't I Read the Zodiac?

One day at work my buddies and I thought we should question the relevance of a man's zodiac sign, and whether or not it would make him a compatible choice for us. The truth is this. The zodiac is right. I looked up at least three of the men I had long term relationships with, and read their sign to myself, only to find out each and every one of them had the characteristics of their zodiac sign. Some make good partners for your sign, others may be horrible.

Aries men are strong family men. They love to work hard. They love to keep us safe, and they love their partners and family. These men need women who are strong and energetic. These men are very loyal and will stick by you through the tough stuff, if you have the pizzazz to keep up with them. I dated an Aries man for many years. He was strong and wonderful, and his family meant the world to him. He knew how to work hard, loved his parents, and took pride in everything he did. He bought me many gifts, most which at the time I thought were silly, but now that I look back I realize how useful and practical they really were.

Pisces. Well ladies, the Pisces man is quiet and reserved. He may need you to make the first move, as he is quite shy. He can be kind and thoughtful, and often tends to take interest in making the relationship work. He is a good catch. He likes to love. He likes women. And he is a good choice. And damn it, I have never dated a Pisces!

The Sagittarius man – oh how I wish I read the zodiac before picking this one. A Sagittarius man is often a charmer, a smart well-educated man, who often enjoys learning. He is fiery and sexy. He can be a bit of a dreamer, with his head in the clouds a bit of the time. Sagittarius men can be selfish. They will keep their eyes open, always looking for the woman that catches his eye. He is impossible to tie down as he is always looking for the next best thing. He is often sexy and plays the part of eye candy for women, making him really hard to commit to a long-term relationship. He is also often afraid of commitment, which is why he often sleeps with one eye open, waiting for the next best thing to walk by, and for him not to miss it. If you do manage to keep and hold onto him, he will be kind and compassionate. He will care for you and nurture you. Sagittarius men want a woman who is sexy and confident and spontaneous. They want a woman who takes good care of themselves, as they likely do the same.

I dated a Sagittarius. Oh, how he was all of these things. He was beautiful, sexy, kind and very hard to hang onto. He never used the word commitment or relationship, as I don't really think he believed in either. He took off on his white horse, faster than I could chase him.

Now that I look back I wish I would have known. I don't want a man I have to chase and fall down chasing. I want a man I can chase, grab onto, and hang onto forever. Move over Sag, there are many more wonderful men out there waiting for me. Get out your laptop and start looking. There is some truth in the zodiac, and we just need to be open to it.

All The King's Horses

It seems as though as I get older and continue dating, I have learned that men's values and goals get more clear. A lot of men in their forties who are single now, or are divorced, have a very strong work ethic. It's as though they are driven by status. They are driven by accomplishment. They are forced to work harder than most, because they have to. Some pay child support. Some pay several people child support. Some struggle to exist, because of their child care commitments.

I admire these men. They are strong and they are dedicated. They sacrifice so many of the pieces of their lives, so that their children are cared for and happy. They sacrifice a lot of their time to work harder than most, and work thousands of miles away from home, for weeks at a time, in order that they provide for their children.

It's all the King's horses. Men are driven to work hard. They are driven to care for their partner and their families. And they take pride in caring for us. That's something we should take pride in, a man who cares about us, and is willing to sacrifice some part of themselves in order to provide for us.

A man who works hard is important. A man who loves his family and children is important. It's beautiful to me. I do not expect any man to sacrifice any part of themselves for me, but I find it so very beautiful to see a man who is willing to work hard to make a difference. They are good men. And they are the horses that keep the kings happy.

Find that man, the one who works hard, the man who still finds time for you, the one who makes your heart beat faster every day on your way home from work. Find the man who wants to be a good man for you.

Viva Las Vegas

Thanks to a very dear friend, I finally got to Vegas. I don't know actually how many times she pressured me to go, but it took so many I lost count. She was determined that I needed to get there, and that I would love life in the glow of the big city.

I agreed to go the summer of 2015. I found the noise and speed to which traffic and people walked down the streets overwhelming, but I couldn't help but feel the buzz that everyone gets walking that first step out of your hotel room onto the strip. Your heart starts pounding so quickly you just know that there's no turning back.

Tess had bought us tickets to a UFC night, packed with all the fixings, including free draft beer, and a guaranteed room full of hot boys and testosterone. I agreed to go, first because I love boxing, and second because I knew there would be a lot of single men there and I was single.

As we entered the pub on the strip, and found our last-minute seats in the room, I looked around to find a room full of gorgeous, pumped, athletic men waiting patiently for the fights to begin. I couldn't help but feel their energy and began to drink, perhaps a bit more quickly than I should have.

The fights began, and I couldn't believe how many men love to see women fight. Each round of the fights, Tess and I drank a few more drinks. A few more drinks turned into way too many, and we met our first round of boys. They were Canadian, and asked if we wanted to join them for the rest of the night following the fights, to cruise the Las Vegas strip. We agreed to join them, and so the night, or part two of it, began.

We cruised the strip and ended up at a restaurant, which for the life of me at the time, I could not remember the name of. I knew it sounded like peanut butter and jam, or something like that, but wasn't really worried about it, until I decided to go to the washroom and found myself lost in Vegas. I was so excited by the lights and music on the strip, I walked outside to take a peek at what was going on, and within seconds I was lost. I couldn't find peanut butter and jam, and I had left my purse and phone and room key at the table with Tess. "Gee whiz," I thought, I wasn't any more grown up now than I was ten years ago.

I began walking down the strip to try and find my hotel. We stayed at a nice hotel and I knew I only had two choices in order to find it, walk to the left or the right. But I knew that I could be walking an hour in the wrong direction, and two hours once I realized and turned around, and all I wanted to do was lie on the strip and sleep. I kept walking, trying not to look conspicuous.

As I so obviously emitted a look of fear on my face, and probably an overwhelming stupor of drunkenness, a handsome young man walked up beside me and asked if I was okay. As I cautiously told him I was fine, he introduced himself to me, and I instantly asked if he was a killer. As funny as that sounds, at the time, I thought there was no point in beating around the bush. His name was Jack and he was Canadian. He must be safe and okay to walk with, or so I thought.

As we talked and I continued down the strip with him, he offered to walk me to my hotel. My heart knew that I was being silly, but I thought I had nothing else to lose – I could either sleep on the strip, or get walked home by a hunk, who may or may not murder me on the way.

He walked me to the hotel and gave me a very light kiss on the cheek. He asked if I would be okay and went on his way. I begged hotel staff to let me in my room, by showing them my passport for I.D., and quickly fell asleep in my bed.

Tess returned to the room a few hours later, informing me that she had waited at peanut butter and jam for several hours. Needless to say, with a bit of dark humor, she was very angry with me. I didn't care at the time. I was so drunk, all I cared about was getting my drunk ass to bed.

The next morning I woke to take my spinning head and body to the bathroom. I had created my own movie, which I wasn't proud of, and had a very dark walk of shame waiting for me that day. I walked into the bathroom and found a business card for a DJ in Montreal. I didn't remember getting a business card from anyone, but later realized that this was the card from Jack. He had walked me home, and God knows how he spoke at the end of the night, but he got me home safely and he gave me his card. I quickly emailed the address on the card, as I was completely grateful he got my sorry drunk ass home in one piece.

Jack met me at the pool that day, and I instantly fell in love with him. He was built like a running back football player, and had a laugh that you couldn't help but giggle when you heard it. He was kind, funny and smart and he was going to be flying home that night. We spent the day singing and dancing in the pool, and then met for supper and drinks, before his flight home.

I remember sitting in Margaritaville, waiting for him to arrive. He walked in and had brought me a gift, his tee shirt, that smelled of his cologne, and told me that he didn't want to go home. He wanted to stay to get to know me, and didn't know what I had done to him in such a short time that made it hard for him to leave.

Jack went home that night. We texted and emailed for months, but never seemed to cross paths again. I packaged up a memoir of Vegas and mailed it to him shortly after my trip. He was flattered, to say the least, and I believe I took a bit of his heart with me, like he had taken a little piece of mine.

I still think of my DJ, and how he rocked my world in less than 24 hours. He touched my heart and recharged my faith in love, living life to the fullest, and taking chances. We still talk and I often tell people about how we met, and they think I'm crazy that I never got my butt to Montreal to see him, to find out why this happened.

Things happen for a reason. Maybe someday our paths will cross again and we will giggle and laugh and touch each other's hearts the way we did at the pool that day in Vegas. Thank you DJ for instilling faith in me that life is about taking chances, that things happen for a reason and that they didn't say Viva Las Vegas for nothing. Vegas is the life. Viva Las Vegas!

What Does Your Heart Say?

I have a picture that hangs on my bathroom wall. Everytime I struggle to find an answer to something, I ask myself "what does my heart say?" It works every time. Too many times, we forget to listen to our guts, to what our heart is telling us, to the little signs that make us uncomfortable.

Have you ever lied in bed with someone and struggled to fall asleep? Have you ever struggled with the silence in the dark, because it was so awkward. Have you ever struggled with a kiss because it felt like there was no passion, like the man you were kissing was absent, that he didn't feel your passion?

Well I think those are signs of faith. If you kiss someone and they don't kiss you back, perhaps they are not reciprocating something because they don't feel the same. Have you ever hugged someone but felt a squirmy return, while your heart soars with love and their return feels cold and ugly?

I fully believe that a person who loves you, or feels passion or love for you, will not be able to hide their feelings from you. Their kiss will feel full, their passion will be felt in their hug, in their skin, in their eyes. Silence will not be awkward. It will be peaceful, and bring you solace.

Believe in yourself. Believe in your heart. What your heart says is often what it wants your head to believe. If we struggle with someone and feel they are cold or empty or lacking the passion in their kiss, their touch, or their attention, they likely aren't right for you. Your heart knows what it needs. We need to listen to it.

Desperately Seeking Shania

The conversation started when Shania Twain, "Man I feel like a Woman", played on the radio. I quickly blurted out that I didn't care for the song (no offense Shania!), and the conversation turned from silly to serious.

It's a song. It's not Shania. It's always been a great song to me, but I guess I have just heard it too many times. I don't have to like it, or need to tap my toes when the song comes on the radio. But when I was asked why I wasn't crazy about the song, I quickly responded I simply didn't like it. When I was asked if I was jealous, or if I felt threatened by Shania and her beauty, I sat in disbelief that someone would ask me such a silly question.

"Am I jealous", I asked myself? No, I am not. Am I jealous she has millions of dollars that I don't? No, I'm not. Am I jealous of Shania herself, or something about her that I wish I had? No, I'm not. Shania, you are beautiful, you are a role model for many of us, but I don't need to be envious of you, and feel the need to be just like you, in order to make me feel complete.

The question then becomes this. Why do men think that women want to be someone else? Why do they think that we need to have another's person's looks, their bodies, their booty, their breasts, their fame, their clothes, their lifestyle or their money? I, in particular, do not feel insecure or threatened by anyone. I like who I am, and I defend that whenever someone questions my self-esteem. I don't want to be anyone else. I don't want their hair or their body, or their money, and I like who I am.

I guess then we have to look at the bigger picture. If a person wants you to be someone else or thinks you need to be like someone else, then they aren't for you. If they make you feel silly or stupid, or like you just aren't good enough, then the only person who is not good enough is them.

I then responded "why, do you have Shania waiting on the sidelines?", as I thought about the silliness of the nature of his comments. Of course, he didn't. Did he have anyone on the sidelines waiting to be dated that looked anything like Shania? Of course, he didn't. He used this tool to make me feel small and insecure, but failed.

I love who I am and I have taken many years to feel confident enough to stand up for myself. I think I am beautiful inside and out, and will never let a man take my self-esteem away from me. Neither should you. Be proud of who you are and your own beauty. Don't envy anyone else and try really hard to fall in love with you. No one can love you the way you can.

And for those men out there who want to date Shania, I wish you all the best. I am pretty sure Shania is married or taken, happy in her own life, and certainly not looking for you. Keep reaching for the stars that you may never reach, and for your own inner struggle to make women feel insecure.

And ladies, remember this. Women rock, and there is beauty in each and every one of us. One of my very dear male friends said that to me, and it's something I really believe and will never forget. If a man is looking for Shania, well tell him to keep on looking. Be you. Be proud. Be strong. The man who loves you just because you are you is out there, and he will love you like you love yourself. Beauty is internal and a good man will see that. Xo

Rearview Mirrors

Rearview mirrors are for checking your hair, for watching for cars, to keep from running people over. Stop looking back girl. You cannot move forward to see all those great things waiting, if you keep looking behind you at the past.

I can't count how many times I have used a rearview mirror in a new relationship. Instead of looking forward, looking to the future, and giving a new person the chance to know me, I spend most of my time thinking about that last guy, the one who stole my heart, the one who broke it. I never gave so many of my dates that fresh start, my full attention, my whole heart. I was looking in the mirror, hoping my Mr. Wrong would run up behind me and rescue me, tell me he was sorry, that he made a mistake. But the truth is, he never did. He was behind me for a reason. He wasn't meant to be, he wasn't into me, and he was behind me because he was not supposed to be in my life, or in my future.

So ladies, please stop looking back. Things do happen for a reason. The right guy will come into your life, enter it with passion and enthusiasm, and he will stick around. He won't walk ahead of you. He won't leave you behind. He will walk beside you. He will take you with him. And he will be in your life today, just like he was yesterday. If he stands in your past, in the background, behind the car in a memory where you only remember the good stuff, he's probably exactly where he is supposed to be.

Look in the mirror. You are beautiful. You deserve more. You have so much in the future to be excited about. Rearview mirrors are for looking behind you, and not looking forward. Focus on the future and what could be, rather than what could have been. When you are truly happy, you will know why things happen the way they do.

How Many Suitcases?

It's funny. Countless times and emails on dating websites, guys have commented about other girls they have met online. How they had too much baggage, how their kids took up too much of their time, or how their exes were crazy. Every story has two sides. Every person has a suitcase. Every person has issues. Choosing to believe that we are an exception is foolish. Each person has a suitcase. Each person has a story.

I don't come right out now and ask how many suitcases a person has, and frankly that may be a bit offensive. But I do ask what they have thought of the people they have met while dating, and see how they respond. If they say everyone has baggage and no one has what they are looking for, then I truly believe they are the ones carrying the biggest suitcase.

I guess it's pretty simple. Everyone has a suitcase and baggage and a closet full of surprises. Only a few will come out of the closet and open their suitcase to show you what is inside. Some will chose to hide their suitcases, keep the closet door shut, and to pretend they are the perfect catch.

Baggage is good. It tells a story. Each one of us has lived a life and has had a purpose. One suitcase may have your kids in it. Another may have your parents and siblings in it. Another may have your work worries in it. Another may have a whole bunch of exes who you decided you would never let out of the suitcase again. Others may have your deepest, darkest secrets that only you will ever know. And, you know what, that's okay. Nobody is perfect. We all have our angels and our demons. Baggage is good. If you didn't have any, you would not have lived.

Don't ever let anyone make you feel you are not worth their time, that you have too much baggage, or that you are too much work. If they are good people and they deserve to be in your life, they will accept you, your suitcases, your children, your family and the life you have created. Be proud of who you are and feel blessed that you have suitcases. If you didn't, you would not have a story to tell, or a history of wonderful family, friends, children, parents, lovers, idols and heros and then you wouldn't be able to say you truly lived a life that was full and complete.

Crazy

I once met a man who said that all women are crazy, and to some extent I couldn't help but agree with him. He whispered "I like crazy", and we giggled, as if it was something we needed to hide or pretend we didn't really believe in.

We talked about crazy dating stories. He spoke of women that he had dated who started out "normal", and then turned a bit sideways crazy, and some who broke his wallet, others who broke his heart. Others who had him arrested, others who drove him crazy, then vanished, and others who made him believe that all women are crazy.

I think we do have a bit of crazy in all of us. It's a crazy that makes us think we deserve the best, a crazy that makes us do things to protect ourselves when we feel we have been hurt or taken advantage of.

I don't think crazy is a bad thing. "Am I crazy", I wondered? And my response was yes, maybe I am. Crazy for falling for a lot of people who had no intention of investing anything in my life or my world, and crazy for saying horrible things to them, when they chewed up or stomped on my heart.

I think we are all a bit crazy. But to tell you the truth I think men like us that way. We entertain them, we scare them a little, and we keep them on their toes. Crazy can be sexy. We need to have fun and sometimes be crazy. Crazy can be inspiring. It can make us live on the edge. It can make us take chances that most others wouldn't. Sometimes it makes us feel alive.

Don't be afraid to be you, or to show the man in your life who you really are and what makes you tick. I love the fact I am a bit eccentric, I like to fart and giggle and talk about silly things. I love who I am. And I love the fact that some men love "crazy", and I have had the opportunity to meet them. Cheers to crazy. Xo Tennessee.

Next

It is quite funny. My longest relationship was eleven years. It seems that each relationship after that got progressively shorter, or at the very least, my patience for each one of them decreased.

My long term relationship and marriage lasted eleven years. Each one of those years, however, seemed to be another year or opportunity, in my mind, that the relationship would get better, that we would learn to like each other again and learn to communicate. Truth is, it didn't happen. And although I stayed as long as I did, it didn't get any better.

My next relationship lasted two years, two amazing, fun, incredible years. I truly felt I loved him and that he was the one. We spent many hours and days together, reassuringly confirming for me that he was the one, that he felt the same, that this was it. Until the day that he told me while we were driving in the car that he wasn't sure he wanted a relationship.

"What", I asked myself, "isn't this a relationship"? After two years I thought, how was it that he just realized that? As angry as I got at the time, I realized that he never did want a relationship. He just wasn't being honest with me. He always said he was honest and I guess in a sense he was. I just never asked the right questions. And to be honest, he was right. I never did come out and ask if he wanted a relationship.

My next relationship lasted eight months. They were eight crazy, fun, sensational, goosebump creating months, where I thought this guy loves me, this guy is great, this guy can't possibly let me go. Until the day when he said he didn't want a relationship. Again, I forgot to ask the right questions. And he was right. I just never asked the right questions. And in the end I was the one who got blindsided.

So my point is this. I didn't ask the right questions. I was naïve in the fact that I thought the people I dated felt the same way that I did. I believed they were crazy about me, couldn't wait to see me again, and would do anything for me, because that is how I felt. Of course they didn't have to, they have their own personal feelings. And that is not always what you sense, or what you see.

So, as time goes by, each time I meet a new person and enter into a new relationship, my patience level, or period to which I allow a person to tell me they don't want a relationship, has gone from eleven years to approximately eleven days. Yes, eleven days. My patience has diminished and it's like an assembly line. If you are not willing to invest in me, well next I say, I am ready to meet the next best thing.

We all need to remember that life opens all kinds of doors for us. We can chose to open each door, and we can also chose to close them. We can like what we see inside that door, or we can pretend to believe that we do. Either way, we have many choices in the world. One door closes and many others will open. Hang in there too. Keep the doorways free of clutter and hazard-free, and you just may find the door that leads to the love of your life. I am still hopeful he's out there. I just know he is. And if it takes meeting several men before then, I am better equipped to say "next", when they do not meet my expectations or have the same long term plans that I do.

The Depot

I call it the depot. It's like guys think they can drive by the depot, make a deposit, show up anytime.

"The depot", you ask, "what is it?" Well, it's what I call the place where a guy who thinks he can pop into and out of your life at any time he choses, goes. He can vanish for a month, not answer your texts, then suddenly out of the blue thinks he can pop into the depot again, without any explanation as to where he has been, and why he showed up now.

It's a text late at night, it's a text asking "can I come and cuddle", or a conversation that says all the right things, but you know you're likely going to chat for awhile and then end the conversation and never see the guy again. That guy will stop into the depot whenever your open sign is lit up, and he will leave the depot without any desire to look back. No commitment. No strings attached.

The depot? It's a warm cozy bed when a guy needs a safe place to land. It's a nice warm conversation, over an ice cold beer, when their aunt passes away, or their father is diagnosed with cancer. The depot is technically always open, if you have 24-hour access and unlimited services. I think guys need and love to have a depot. They pop in when they need to, they get what they want and they leave. It is simple I guess. Guys are different. They want a hands free, no-commitment, hassle-free guarantee that you are always going to be there for them. Period.

So, what can we do to prevent the depot from being short-staffed? Well we can only be open during certain hours. We can avoid having any sales, or falling for any salesmen who have all the right pitches. The depot is your own. You can chose to be open late hours. It can be open for anyone who wants you to be open, or it can only be available when you chose it to be.

You have to love yourself first, and I really believe that. You can't possibly get the respect you deserve, if you don't love and respect yourself first. Believe in greatness. Expect greatness. Expect the guy is going to make an effort and love you the way you would love them. If you don't, the depot is always open, and the door will always keep revolving. Close the door. Have restrictions. Don't have sales. Just have good solid values and rules, and you will get the respect you desire and deserve.

Trust that if you stick to your guns, hold onto your values, and hold out for the guy who will make the effort, that you will find the guy who makes all your dreams come true. He's out there. He has to be. And I highly doubt he is standing in the bus depot tonight, waiting for someone else. He is waiting for you. Now get out there and find him.

Victoria's Secret

Well I can't tell you how many times I have wondered what her secret is. The image, the commercials, the beautiful bodies that walk the catwalk wearing wings and scantily clad outfits, reaching out to the depths of men, to their souls, to their dirty little minds.

I can't tell you how many thousands of dollars I have spent on their clothing. I don't know if it is sexier to me to just buy the lingerie and feel like a million bucks in it, or if it's more about the thrill of the store, the thrill of the chase, the thought of the look on my boyfriend's face when he sees me in my new clothes.

The truth is, I have bought bras for tonnes of dollars. I have a million pairs of panties. I own all kinds. I have tried thongs. I have tried cheekies. I have even worn granny panties, for those not too romantic nights when I am home alone and could care less what my underwear looks like. For the sake of sexy, I have worn thongs and spent the entire time wearing them trying to pull them out of my butt.

Well, the answer is simple. I did it to feel sexy, for the thought that once I put on these crazy little pieces of underwear that the man I was dating would be so in love with me, he would tear off my clothes, think I was the sexiest woman alive, and beg me to buy more.

Well I learned this the hard way. Guys don't pay attention to the type of underwear you are wearing. They just want to take it off. They don't ooh and awe and ogle over the scantily clad outfit you spend hundreds of dollars on. They simply don't. They just want to take the damn outfit off and get you into bed. No delay, no time to look at it, they simply don't care.

So miss Victoria, what then is your secret? I think deep down that your secret is wonderful. You inspire women to feel beautiful and sexy. You inspire us to be better, to dream big, to think that the world is full of men who will appreciate us and the kinds of clothing we pay so much money for, all in the name of sexy.

Victoria, thank you for making sexy acceptable, for allowing women to feel valued and beautiful, and for helping us to feel good about ourselves when sometimes the world doesn't help with that. Victoria's Secret is about you. You are beautiful and sexy. You do not need a man to make you feel beautiful. Put on your new undies and dance around the house, feel like you are wearing wings, that you are the most beautiful woman in the world. Feeling sexy is about you, not about a man.

Plain Jane

You know it's all about being comfortable in your own skin. Not worrying about a façade, or an image of something you wish you could be.

Be yourself. Be you. And be proud and excited about that person that will love you just the way you are. Be brave. Be confident. And take pride in who you really are. We are all beautiful just the way we are. And like my Auntie Joyce, bless her beautiful heart, always preached, don't ever try to be somebody, because you already are.

I remember being in junior high and feeling much less than pretty. I had pimples and oily skin, a wave in my red hair that I hated, and giant boobs that just seemed to grow overnight. I was getting ready to go to a school dance, and I think my mom saw my insecurity. I didn't wanna go. I felt ugly and was shy and nervous, and worried about my red hair and oily skin, when my mom quickly responded with "you will be the best looking one there". As I put on my shoes, I remember how my confidence grew. And although I felt really ugly and afraid, my heart knew I was beautiful. Thank you Mom for helping me to become the confident woman that I am today.

Tell your kids they are beautiful, and they will look in the mirror and believe that they are. Beauty is within, and it's something each of us need to learn to feel and be. When you walk into a room believe you are beautiful, and tell yourself that. Tell your kids that, and I promise they won't forget it.

As a result of this, I decided while being single that I needed a new approach to dating. I wanted to be myself. I wanted to find a good man that loved me for who I am, not just for my physical appearance. I started going on dates with men in my plain clothes - no earrings, not a stitch of makeup on. I felt a bit awkward on that first date, but after going on a date with two different people and not caring what I looked like, I had the best time and they seemed to have few complaints. They said I was cute and that's all I needed. I could save dressing up, wearing earrings, and looking sexy for another time. After all, wouldn't they be surprised to see how well I could dress up after seeing me as my natural self.

So ladies, be yourself, be free and be proud. Find a man who loves your heart. Remember you are somebody, and you need to love yourself before someone else will. You are nothing less than beautiful.

Red

Dear ladies, here it goes. I have fought all my life with my red hair. I have loved it, hated it, and loved it again. I have spent many years of my adult life coloring my hair so I could avoid it. But let's face it, after years and bottles of hair dye, I am a redhead. There's nothing I can do about it. I have come to terms with it and I love it.

I think people really fight to be something else. I think we try to be something we think other people find attractive, or what the latest status quo reigns as beautiful. But when it comes down to the point of it all, we truly are beautiful when we are ourselves.

Since I have been single, my hair has been many colors. It has been brown, dark brown, chocolate brown, nearly black, and on occasion, my true-blue red. I have had more luck now with my natural color than I have had in any situation in the past.

Little did I know my new nickname by a random stranger was now "Red". He noted in his very first conversation that he loved my red hair, and that if we ever met and became friends, he would call me Red. On another occasion, I had no idea if what I was presenting as was the type of person he was looking for. My picture showed my red hair, but when I showed up without a stitch of makeup and rosy cheeks and red hair, I was doubtful that I would hear from him again.

I quickly heard from him following our first date, although I figured I wouldn't, and he later admitted that he always found red-headed women to be some of the most beautiful women in the world. He also said that he had never dated a red head before, and was smitten by the thought of that. Not only was I flattered, but I was excited. After all, what woman wouldn't want a man who thinks she is beautiful?

I guess my point is this. Guys don't care what color your hair is. They want you to be yourself and they can choose what it is they are looking for. They can hen peck their "type", or try to make you something you aren't, or they can chose to love you just the way you are. I am currently flattered and love my new name. Red is perfect. Red is who I am. And Red is who I am going to be. I hope you can find the person you really are, and shine bright. Be yourself and be proud. Other people will see your beauty and the beauty of feeling good in your own skin.

Yours truly,
Red

Perfect

The old saying it is. Nobody's perfect and they certainly aren't. I know I'm not perfect, so why in the world would I expect to find a man who is? It's simple. I cannot think that I will find perfect, because perfect does not exist.

It is funny how we set such high standards for people, when we know deep down inside ourselves that our expectations of others are not realistic. Have you ever dated someone that you thought was beautiful? Have you ever looked back and thought that that person's beauty was more than surface? Their beauty was skin deep, it was beauty that came from within.

Well I have. I remember very clearly dating a man who I loved more than anything. I was in university and we met there. He was charming and funny, and always made me laugh so hard I would get a pain in my stomach. We would drive to the car wash, and I would find more joy in something as simple as washing the car, than I did going on a trip to Vegas. He made me laugh, he made me smile, and I loved him more than anything for that.

Now that I look back I realize that he wasn't beautiful or gorgeous, or perfect in any way. But he was perfect for me. He was full of spirit and had a heart full of joy and love, and he brought me so much happiness I am forever grateful for that.

As I am now older I can admit to myself, perhaps I never did that before, that nobody is perfect. And, I also know for a fact that I don't want someone who is. I want someone who is perfect for me. Someone who makes me laugh and smile and who when I look at them makes me feel like the luckiest girl in the world.

So ladies, perfection is all in the eyes of the beholder. Perfect is how you define it. Perfect is something that we strive to find. Perhaps you and I both need to focus on truly searching for someone perfect for nobody else but us.

Keep searching. Never settle for less than you deserve. Remember that you aren't perfect, and that searching for someone who is will be an endless task. Find the one that is perfect for you and enjoy, appreciate and treasure your moments with him.

Xo

It Had To Be You

Have you ever wondered why you meet someone? Why you dated someone and it didn't work out, why in the world the love of your life walked out? Well, I think to myself, it had to be you.

We meet different people at every different stage in our lives. We fall in love when we are 16. We find puppy-love that really is based on friendship, and the idealistic view that our prince will show up one day and carry us away. Truth is, we have hope and faith in the goodness of people and we dream about the perfect relationship, the man that will complete us, the person who will be our better half, and our knight in shining armour.

I know we have all dated monsters. We have all dated princes. And we have all loved and lost at some point in our lives. But if we truly open our minds to the fact that each person taught us something, we can stop dwelling on the past negatively, and be grateful for each blessing that each person teaches us.

It's the guy who walks into your life and treats you like a princess. It's the guy who walks into your life, and you open up and rip out your heart and give it to him, and then he walks away with it. It's the guy who never treated you well, but you loved him so much it felt physically hurtful when he left your life, and left a void that you could not seem to fill again.

Each one of them served a purpose. They teach us what we want. They teach us what we need. And they teach us what we don't want. Each one is introduced to us to teach us something. A lesson, a story, a blessing. And we can chose to see each one of those lessons as a gift, or we can chose to feel like the victim.

I recently talked with my friend about relationships. As much as I had had a few sour ones that ended badly, as I have gotten older I have chosen to see the blessings each one brought to my life. Although each one ended, I learned more about me, what I want and don't want, and have something to compare each of them to.

Some will teach us how to love. Some will teach us compassion and kindness. Some will show us affection and love, and lavish us with heartfelt things that touch us deeply. Others will teach us what we don't want. They will roll over in bed after sex and make you feel like they should have paid you. They will open a door and knock you down to get inside before you. They will not introduce you to their families or children or friends, not because they don't have time, but because they are not the right person for you. They will teach you what you want – to be admired and loved and to be someone that your loved one will want to show off to the world. They will walk beside you and be proud of who you are.

Every person teaches us a lesson. We have to chose to see goodness, even in the worst of situations or in the worst of endings. It had to be you. Each person has a purpose. You may not know it while you are in the relationship, but if you look back and try to see things in a positive light you will feel relief in knowing the gifts. You can use those gifts in future relationships and to learn more about you.

Remember next time you meet someone that they are here for a reason. They are here to teach you something. They will teach you something about you, something about life, and something about why we are all here on this Earth, trying to sort it all out and make sense of it all. Enjoy every minute for its value. Appreciate it and enjoy it. It had to be you.

Who's The Lucky Guy?

I remember standing against the wall one night, while out in a bar in my town. It was dark and dingy, but for some reason we often frequented it for the music, and the occasional crazy crowd the bands would bring in.

At the time I was seeing a man I was smitten with. He was beautiful and charming, and always said the right thing. He would take care of me, cover me up in the morning when he left for work, and would put socks on me during a movie, when he thought my feet were cold. I loved him more than I had loved anyone, and felt very lucky to have him in my world.

While standing against the wall that night, reading texts that he was sending me, it was as though I had not a care in the world. It was as if I was in the middle of a wonderful, crazy place but had no idea what was going on around me, because I was smitten with the man that I was talking to. His words meant more to me than anything, as I stood oblivious to the world around me.

A man walked up to me while I was looking down at my phone and, as I looked up said, "who's the lucky guy?" I smiled a bit of a devilish and guilty grin, saying "no one", perhaps portraying the image of being offended by his comments. The messages kept coming, and I continued my oblivion to the world. It took me years to figure out what that guy meant that night, but when I finally figured out what he was saying, I had to just shake my head.

What he was saying was that whoever I was talking to put a twinkle in my eye, a skip in my step, and a confidence that the rest of the world couldn't help but take notice of. I was the luckiest girl in the world at that moment, and the rest of the world knew it. At the time, I didn't know it, but now I do.

Girls, we have to keep searching for the man who puts the sparkle in your eye, and a twinkle in your heart. A man who, no matter where you are, can send you a message or a few words that will override the importance of anything you are engaged in.

I guess the world knew it that night and I was hopeful that I had that lucky guy and he was all mine. Unfortunately, we didn't work out, as I am sure you determined, however, I am grateful for the love and joy that he gave me while we were dating. I respect the things that he taught me and the grace in being able to show the world how good that felt. Keep on searching until you find it.

Laughter Is The Best Orgasm

Have you ever sat with friends and laughed so hard you realize that your search for romance and the man of your dreams is just silly?

Well as I sat with my girlfriends in a local pub, friends I hadn't seen in ages, I realized just that. There is nothing like laughter, a really hard belly laugh that is contagious. It makes you laugh and wakens your spirit. It wakes every ounce of everything inside you that may have been lying dormant.

We began to share dating stories. Some were unbelievable, others were nightmares, and regardless of their nature, most of them were hilarious and burst us into tears of laughter. We began comparing dating sites that we had been on, comparing men that we had chatted with, and began swiping each picture on the dating site my friend was on.

As the phone lit up, and the room in the pub was quite small, we noticed a few faces on the site that looked like patrons in the bar. As we giggled and laughed and passed the phone around, we noticed a profile picture of a man who appeared to look like the guy who was seated behind us. As we turned the phone to him to show him, the room watched in surprise.

He walked closer to the table and giggled with us. We asked if the profile was his and he giggled, refusing to tell us if it was or wasn't. He returned to his table and the night continued as I swiped the phone again and again, each time with a giggle, as the room began to take part in our search.

The table beside us, with two women and two men, began to catch on and were familiar with the site, and joined in on our fun. They cheered as we swiped, saying "swipe left", "swipe right", and we laughed as we scanned the room to see how many of the men on the site were actually in the room with us. The room was small, but the laughter was contagious. We had won everyone's heart, as they watched our joy in searching for the one, and they joined in on our laughter.

I guess what I realized that night was that we all want to be happy. We all want to find the one who makes our hearts whole, and the one who makes us feel like we are special and that we are loved. We also want to be happy and thrive in an environment where we are safe and loved, and free to enjoy the minute of the moment. There is nothing like laughter. Enjoy it and remember, laughter is the best orgasm.

The Five-Minute Rule

Okay, we all know the guy. He is obsessed with his phone. It's almost glued to his hand, stuck to his face on his pillow when he is sleeping, it sits on the table while you are out for a romantic dinner, and it's constantly a piece of electronics to which he devotes a huge amount of his time. I know the guy. He has the phone hooked to his pants. It sits beside his head or on his bedside table. He hides the phone in his pocket, so obviously afraid you may see who he has been talking to. It's the guy who hides the phone in his pocket when he is with you, rather than placing it on the table.

I have developed my own five-minute rule. It's sort of like the quote "maybe he's just not that into you". We all know the drill. If you send a tough question to a guy and have any kind of bad feeling that he maybe just isn't that into you, and he doesn't answer right away, well I think he either doesn't want to answer, doesn't care if he answers, or he just doesn't know what to say. The guy who leaves you hanging, and refuses to answer your questions, needs to follow the five-minute rule.

If you see him at the table, lying in bed, at work, in his car, or just about anywhere with the phone glued to his hand, in a panic to answer every text within the first minute of receiving it, he needs to pass the five-minute rule. Don't tell him about it, just keep it in the back of your head. If you send him a text or ask him a question and he doesn't answer for a day, well that is a pretty good indication that he failed the test. He is not interested or invested, and you need to keep on moving. Get back on-line, go on other dates, and realize that there are other guys out there that will answer your questions, feel responsible to answer your questions, and can be honest enough to tell you when they do not know what to say or that they are afraid they are going to hurt or offend you.

Same goes for us, I guess. If a guy messages us and you don't care to answer and don't feel an inkling of guilt for leaving them hanging, well then you failed the five-minute rule. Be honest to yourself. You aren't interested. They deserve more. Be honest and tell them and move on.

Dear Bud Light,

Dear bud light, last night we reconnected again. The night started out with you and I thinking we had great ideas. You provided the drinks and I enjoyed the laughs and the comraderie, and the night began like it usually does.

One Bud Light, one Bud Light, two. Whatever happened a few hours later is a bit of a blurr. I had a great time but every time you brought me another drink I decided to make some decisions that I normally never would have.

Oh, the taste of a good beer. Each one went down so smooth and the laughs became more evident with the passing hours and the second, third and fourth beer. Our friendship changed a bit later, when I realized I had the courage I needed to make some bad decisions.

I invited myself to my new friend's home. It was wonderful and crazy and each laugh and conversation seemed to flow easier and more quickly. We ended up in a hot tub, which for some reason made us feel very thirsty and perhaps dehydrated. We of course had a few more of you and ended up falling asleep pretty quickly.

Dear Bud Light, you crazy little beer. You always start out with good intentions, but then you pressure me to make bad choices. I do make them. I do enjoy them. But when I wake up with my basketball head and a crazy hangover, reminiscing about the crazy night you and I created the night before, well I just want to thank you for that.

You are crazy, you are peer pressure, you are laughter. You guarantee courage, and a basketball head after we spend too much time together. But thank you for giving me the courage that I needed to meet a new friend, spend the evening with belly laughs and giggles, and the opportunity to enjoy life to the fullest. You rock Bud Light. Thank you.

Xoxoxo, Tennessee.

All I Want Is You

I never understood why when you find someone to fall in love with, all of the people who used to be in your dating life chose to show up. They flaunt themselves, flirt with you, and try all kinds of tactics to get back into your life.

I think I have thought about why this happens so many times I have finally sorted it all out. Men find us attractive when we feel good about ourselves, when we are confident, and comfortable in our own skin. We are beautiful regardless, but we are even more beautiful when we know what we want and feel good in our own skin.

Truthfully, I know that glow that a girl gets when she is happy and when she is in a relationship with someone who is good for her. She smiles more, and glows when she talks about that person, showing the rest of the world she is okay and happy, and that is what brings the rest of the world to us.

I truly believe that things happen for a reason. When you meet the right person, you will know that feeling, that glow, that joy, and the rest of the world will see it. Others will flock to you because they also feel your joy, and I believe they will want to also be a part of it.

So girls, when you meet that guy, enjoy him. Feel lucky for just knowing him. Feel grateful for his blessing in your life, and be confident in knowing that all he wants is you.

Firsts

I always told myself there were all kinds of "firsts", as I call them, or things in which the first time they happened would tell me that I had found the one. I guess it was a list of things that I had told myself were special, or at the very least special to me, and would be that sign that I needed to know he was the one.

My first "first", was him being in a room full of people and all he saw was me. Julia Roberts, or a Victoria Secret model, would walk by and he would notice them, but he would turn his head towards me and let me know that he was grateful for me. He would not look at other women with temptation, he would notice their beauty as I also do, but he would look at me with gratitude and appreciation for my own gifts.

My second "first", was a man who says "ditto". Every woman, or is it just me and my sappiness, would fall for a man who blessed a woman's heart with the word. It brings pure joy and romance with that very moment in Dirty Dancing when Patrick Swayze tells Demi Moore how much he loves her, without saying a word, by replying "ditto".

My third "first", would be a man who gives me his tee shirt, a tee shirt that he loves, a tee shirt that he wears to bed and considers to be part of his treasures. It will smell like his skin and the scent of his cologne and I will wear it to bed and dream of him.

My fourth "first", is a man who has read my first book. He would be proud of me for writing the book, and he would have attended my book signing and been proud of me for my accomplishment. He would have taken the time to read my book and would tell me what he thought of it.

Well, if you're out there mister, I am waiting. I have heard the word ditto, but only from one man. By the time I finish writing this book, I will let you know if he turned out to be the one. He also has my book on a table beside his bed. I am not sure if he read it, but at the very least he has it in his hands. He hasn't given me his shirt yet, but I haven't lost hope. If he does, then as crazy as it sounds, I will know that he is the one. I will wear his shirt when I get ready for bed, and he will tell me how much I mean to him, replying "ditto" when I tell him how much I love him. That would be amazing.

Xo, Tennessee.

Cowboy

Have you ever drooled over a cowboy, his jeans, his tight butt, or the swagger that a regular man doesn't have? Whatever it is, it's phenomenal, it's jaw-dropping and it's hot. And I love a great cowboy.

It was New Years Eve, every single woman's dreadful night. I was invited to a few places and dreaded going anywhere, as I was single again and knew the night would be full of people and couples smooching all night in front of me, so much as to make me want to run and hide in the closet until 12:15 a.m.

I accepted the invitation to the party at my friend's house. She was a wonderful friend, the kind who would do anything for you. I knew her party would be amazing, because that's just the kind of person she was, the kind to throw a great party, especially on New Years Eve.

I dressed in my finest. I thought I looked pretty darn good, and wandered into the party, hopeful that some tall, single stranger would scoop me up by midnight. My friend had not mentioned any solos that were going to be there, but nevertheless I was excited about what the night may bring.

The cowboy was in the room. Although he was much younger than I was, I saw him looking at me a few times. He was way too young for me, but hell it was one night that I earned every minute of flirting with him. I smiled back each time his eyes headed my way. He said little, and made a few snide remarks about my age, yet he continued to flirt with me, and I knew I had more control than he thought.

The night moved on quickly and we played board games, had crazy amounts of snacks and beers, and cheered each other at midnight. I felt very lucky to be there, to have a night of fun with one of my very dear friends and to be so blessed with good friends, good food and a wonderful New Years night.

As the night drew closer to an end, I put on my boots on my way to call a taxi and head home. Cowboy quickly stopped me at the door and asked where I was going. He asked how I was getting home and wanted to share the cab ride. I agreed and waited, as he put on his boots and we rode home in the taxi.

Cowboy was a gentleman. He asked to make a pit stop at my house, on the way home, and gave me a good night kiss. He then came into my house for a new years drink and some time to get to know each other. He spent the night and quickly crashed in my bed. Cowboy had a little much to drink and so did I. The sparks, unfortunately, ended at midnight.

In the morning, cowboy woke to realize not only did he spend the night with an older woman, his head was as big as a basketball, and he had no idea where he was. He had no way home. I have never seen a man slide across the floor and shove his boots on faster, in a panic to get home, perhaps to his wife or girlfriend.

The night was amazing. Not because of the cowboy, but because I brought in the new year with great friends. I had met a young cowboy who really didn't do it for me, however, it was what it was and there was nothing I could do to change the outcome of that night.

Cowboy, you were a gentleman until you shared the cab ride home. I will give you that you were pretty darn cute, and much younger than I was, but your swagger wasn't enough to override your ignorance when you left my house the next morning. I have a feeling you weren't a real cowboy, you were just pretending, and I could see right through your vanity and arrogance about being younger than I was.

Cowboy, the point is simple. Putting on cowboy boots does not make you a man. Wearing Wranglers does not make you a better man. And picking up an older woman does not necessarily make you a stud. To tell you the truth cowboy, I was only into you because of your boots.

Xo Tennessee.

Hearts and Angels…
Let's Dance

Danny was one of my favorite dates. He was gorgeous, had a British accent and drove a Lexus. I remember when he met me on our first date and got out of his car. He was gorgeous and his accent made him even cuter than he looked in his pictures. My heart melted with his smile and his wit and his accent. We hit it off immediately.

Danny was perhaps one of the silliest people I have dated. He made me laugh and smile, and could say the silliest of things but made them sound very interesting just by having an accent. After dating for a few months, he offered to have a movie date. I remember he called me before he was coming over, saying how he was so very excited to see me, that he felt like a teenager again. I had butterflies waiting for him to arrive.

We played the British music channel. After all, he was from England and I wanted to make him feel at home. We laughed and danced over a bottle of wine. We sang to songs that we knew from the radio. Then a song we both knew well came on and we began singing and dancing. I have never seen a man dance like no one was watching, but I did that day. He sang out loud and danced around my living room, absolutely unconcerned that I was watching, oblivious to the fact that he was wearing underwear with hearts and angels on them. As we danced around the living room, he told me he had picked out the underwear just for me. They had hearts and angels on them.

We danced, like there was no tomorrow, that night. We laughed. We sang. We texted each other as he stood outside my house having a cigarette. And although we didn't work out in the long term, Danny taught me so many things about life and what it feels like to dance like no one is watching. Perhaps those few hours that night were some of the best I have had while dating. Wherever he is I am sure he is still dancing. Thank you for the inspiration and the dance. You touched my heart and world, probably more than you will ever know.

Mixed-Up Candy

One of the funnest and funniest nights I have had involved spending a few hours with an old flame, who was from Ireland, while out with some girlfriends. We had crossed paths a few times while out in the bars, but were usually too shy to talk about what happened and avoided each other until we had too much drink and had the balls to talk.

This guy was funny. I high-fived him when we talked about the night we met, how he drove me home like we were riding in a race car, like he couldn't wait to get me out of his car. He giggled and laughed, responding that he was probably still drunk from the night before.

We teased each other, laughing at how we met, how the night transpired, how I was wearing a helmet with my Halloween costume, and how he wasn't dressed up in a costume, although I thought he was. He was funny and sweet, and no matter how hard I tried, I could not hold any grudges or have any bad feelings about him.

I guess that's the way it should be. if you had a history, leave it in the past. Enjoy the present and the moment. You only live once, and it's fun to reminisce and to giggle at it. Thank you for the giggles Rory. You were funny when I first met you, and I realize now what attracted me to you. We weren't meant to be but we were meant to be in that moment. You left a pretty good memory in my mind, and a little bit of history that was pleasant. Your accent makes me smile and my attempt to speak with a fake Irish accent that turned out to sound British to you, only made me laugh harder. Thank you for your heart and genuineness. I am glad we have moved on and can be good to each other.

Life's too short to hold grudges. You are a perfect example of the good things that can come out of not holding one. I always thought dating someone from a different country, or mixed-up candy as I called it, would be different. It isn't. They say the Irish are lucky and well, I guess I am lucky that I met you and made a lifelong friend. Cheers to you, to Irish boys, their accents, and our ability to be friends after our relationship failed to work out.

Diving In

I guess it's like diving into the pool that has no water in it. You know you are going to get hurt but you do it anyways. Why? Well because sometimes we do things that we know are going to hurt us, but at the time we think it's worth the risk.

I think the main reason is that little part of us that always keeps us moving, looking for adventure. The little piece of us that tells us to take a chance, live a little, keep moving forward. So often, I know myself, we are afraid to take a chance because we are afraid what will happen, we are afraid we may get hurt, or we would rather be safe than have any regrets. When it comes to matters of the heart and things that make our hearts sing, we often think differently.

I personally am a gambler. Life is a gamble. Life is about taking chances. Playing it safe is awesome, however, sometimes we need to step out on the edge and peek into windows that we otherwise wouldn't dare. Life is pretty straight forward the majority of the time. we go to school, we get an education, we find a career, look for Mr. Right, have a happy family and live happily-ever after. We hope we chose the right path, the right schooling, the right home, the right man and it's not always simple.

I can personally say that I have made alot of crazy choices, and perhaps looked into a few windows that I shouldn't have, but I can say that I took a chance. I have dived into so many pools, it's crazy. Some of the pools had a bit of water in them, others had none at all, and as painful as that was at times, I am glad that I did. I have taken chances on many men, always giving them the benefit of the doubt that they are good people and I have always tried to focus on their good points.

My very dear friend, Jenny often makes fun of me. She says I would never go to the pet store and pick out a healthy puppy. I pick out the undernourished one, the sick one, the shy one, the one with separation anxiety, or the one who is matted and dirty and needs a lot of tlc. Well she's right. I do the same thing with men, or so at least that is what she believes. I am not sure if I agree with her or not, but I do think she has a good point.

So ladies, don't be afraid to go swimming. Take a peek in the pool before you dive in, because more often than not, you can often see what's in front of you, if you chose to keep your eyes open. Wait until the pool has a bit of water and perhaps you should wade in first, before you take a dive. Check the temperature of the water. Look out for sharks and dip your feet in first, before you let any other part of you in it. See what's out there.

Breathe. Take your time. And enjoy every minute of the journey of dating. Pick people who touch your heart and bring you joy. Pick the man who makes your heart skip a beat and puts a skip in your step. And don't write the ending. Let the story write itself and let it unfold the way it is supposed to. Have fun and be safe. Enjoy the ride.

Dearly Beloved,

Well my friends, I often wonder what it takes to make a good marriage, one that is awesome, and that one that will last as long as it's supposed to.

I can count the number of married couples I know who are on their first marriage, are seemingly in love and very happy, and that will likely be together till death do us part. I can also count many people, not on both hands, that are divorced or on their second or third marriage and I presume are very happy the second or third time around.

Perhaps the first time is a test. Maybe it's a test where you figure it all out, where you find out who you really are, and where you fit in a relationship. Perhaps the first time it's the one relationship you don't take seriously, or the one where you give up before you even give it a chance.

I don't know the answer. I haven't been "married" per se, however, I consider my common-law, long-term relationship of over ten years to be a marriage. We lived together, we loved each other, and we had our own family. But here I am, single in my forties, wondering where it all went wrong.

I think back and know that first and foremost, I was immature, I felt that being in a relationship meant that I had to give some part of me up. I believed that marriage meant giving up my identity, my friends, my relationships with other people, my free time and my independence, and I struggled to fight for it.

I was young then. I wanted different things. I wasn't sure where I wanted to be and forever seemed very scary to me. I was young and adventurous, and as much as I loved coming home to someone every day and having a home and a family, I still had to fight for the parts of me that I felt very dearly were threatened.

Now that I am older, and no longer in that long term relationship or marriage, I know what I did wrong. Giving up your life for a relationship is not healthy, and you don't have to do that. If you are in a healthy, solid, loving relationship, you should be able to have friends, to have your own hobbies and free time, and still come home to each other without any worries.

I also wonder this. How many people run to Vegas, get drunk and stupid, meet someone new, and on nothing but a whim head to the chapel to get married? have also wondered how many of these marriages work. How many people wake up the next day or fourty eight hours later and go what the hell have I done? And I wonder how many people run there to get married, find the love of their life, and are still together?

My new project and goal is this. I will head to Vegas. If I am single when I get there, I plan to keep my eyes open to everything. I have met several wonderful people there before, and several who I often thought of years later, wondering what if? No, we didn't get to the altar, nor did we engage in anything other than a beer and a few laughs. But the thought of a couple of them over the years has made me wonder where things would have gone had we pursued each other after our trip.

Dearly beloved. Vegas really is sin city. Perhaps I need to head your way and look for Mr. Right because I sure haven't had many opportunities here. I hope to laugh, giggle and feel the joy of a wonderful night and perhaps a new friend. And if the stars are aligned, perhaps we will head to the altar and tie the knot. You only live once right? So I just may try it.

Dear eHarmony,

I met a very dear friend on this website, two years ago to be exact. He was far away and I didn't imagine we would ever meet or that we would possibly keep in touch. After all, we never met in person and I really didn't expect that I would have developed a wonderful relationship with someone I never met, but I did.

He was sexy and smart and very much a gentleman, from what I could read about him in his messages. His pictures caught my eye, his tattoos, his sexiness, his youthfulness. Our messages began, and they were short and sweet, and a few months passed and I waited for him to vanish. He didn't vanish. He wrote regularly. He was like my pen pal and we were young kids, waiting for each other's messages. He asked about my world, asked about my life, and always responded to my emails as quickly as he could.

Several more months passed, and I kept waiting for him to disappear. After all, what did he have invested in me if we met on a dating site, yet never had any opportunity to meet? The distance was about 900 kms and I certainly wanted to meet him, but had no reliable way of getting there.

Valentine's day passed. He wished me a Happy Valentine's Day. Easter came along and he sent me sweet Easter wishes. Christmas came and went and he made sure he sent me seasons greetings, followed by a Happy New Year.

This happened for two years. He never gave up and he never lost touch. We exchanged pictures periodically, none ever inappropriate and no boundaries on his part were ever crossed. He was a gentleman, and although I never met him, he became a very dear friend.

I never felt sad that we hadn't met. I wondered, however, if we would be the kinds of friends that were still writing years later, like you see in a movie, where people invest in each other on line for a very long time and begin to create something in their minds that really does not exist. I treasured every email. I saved every picture. I asked my little Buddha one day to send me a good man and he did.

I received the email. He said he was coming to a nearby city and that he was going to be coming my way. Again, I didn't expect that we would meet but I was hopeful. I never replied to his note about coming my way, as I didn't want to pressure him or make him feel he had to stop in. He reminded me "I will be coming your way", and noted the day of his arrival in my city. As I gulped and my eyes grew large, I felt a pit in my stomach and a type of nervousness you feel as a teenager, waiting for the love of your life to pick you up for a date. Again, I didn't think he would arrive. But the following day he did.

We met at a nearby hotel. He was gorgeous, just like his pictures. He seemed shy at first. We hugged and felt a bit uncomfortable about the squirminess of meeting in person after two years of my thinking we never would.

We spent the evening drinking beer and sharing great conversation. He remembered every detail of my life and the things that I told him. I felt honored and grateful that he crossed my path, and that I had the chance to make my friendship with this wonderful man a reality. He touched my heart and touched my life.

The clock ticked quickly, and the night passed by and I felt a bit of a pit in my stomach knowing that he would soon leave, to proceed on his journey. Would I ever see him again? Was this beautiful man going to walk into and out of my life in the very same day? And why did I have the kind of butterflies in my stomach that I had never had before? I reminded myself to be strong, that I was grateful that he became real in my world.

Overall I just thanked whoever I needed to, for bringing him into my life. We got to meet, and I believe fully we will keep in touch, and perhaps build a relationship other than friendship, as we had so much in common and such a great time.

Thank you Eharmony, whatever you know about dating that I don't, I sure appreciate. You matched me with a wonderful spirit and a real gentleman and I am every so grateful. You know what you are doing and thank goodness for that.

No Name

I didn't ever think I would get any kind of satisfaction out of knowing that a man who broke my heart would ever try to make his way back into my life. I felt joy in the fact that the guy who broke my heart or hurt me, as a result of not being honest or dragging me along, tried very desperately to find his way back into my heart.

I remember one instance where I received a text. It was a strange text and I had recently bought a new phone and didn't have all of my contacts in it, but I had a feeling that this person was someone who was at one point very dear to my heart.

I am the kind of person who gives everybody a second chance, even if they hurt me, to prove themselves to be the person I thought they were, or to bring joy back into my life. However, if after a second chance they hurt me again they are no longer a priority in my life. I will instantly delete their contact and their phone numbers.

This was the classic case of someone who my gut knew had hurt me. He was a person who wanted to sneak back into my life, although I had given him more than enough chances to be a good person, and they didn't deserve another.

The text started with "hello beautiful", which I knew was not something I would hear from a girlfriend. After all, I had everyone who I considered to be a precious part of my life already in my new phone, however, I used the line that I had gotten a new phone and didn't know who they were.

They refused to say who they were, I am guessing out of embarrassment that I no longer had their information in my phone. I didn't care. I played along. I said that they had the wrong number, and attempted to end the conversation. As persistent as they were, and as curious as I was, I continued to ask questions. They refused to tell me who they were and out of curiosity, I picked up the phone and called the number on my screen.

Nobody answered. It was clear they didn't want to admit that they were thinking of me, or that they were confident that I was still thinking of them. But here we were, once again, with a door slightly open, and a person in the doorway who would not identify themselves to me.

To be funny, I called one of my best friends. I asked her to call the number, and ask the person who answered for the person who I thought it was. She quickly dialed the number and he answered. It was him, the guy who I thought it was, the guy who I had given several chances to prove to me he was a good person, and he failed, each and every time.

He wasn't stupid. He quickly responded in a text that he thought what we did was funny, and I pretended for a bit not to know what he was referring to. I then called him on his antics and asked where he had been. He asked me for coffee and I quickly declined. I told him my heart was somewhere else and reminded him of how he treated me.

I guess the lesson in this is easy to figure out. Once a man breaks your heart, they become a negative place in your mind. For me, they become a vague part of my memory, and nothing but a number that shows up unknown when they call. No name, that is what you are.

Dear so and so, I am sorry that you thought you could stomp back into my life and hoped that my front door would be open. I am happy to say that I have met a very good man and that he treats me better in a short time than you ever did. He is kind and sweet and honest, and even if he is not the one, I am pretty sure from what he has shown me so far that he will tell me the truth. To me, you are now a no-name. I don't think about you, or wish you would come crawling back to me.

As they say, the first time is his fault, the second time is mine. I don't want you back. I never did. I just hadn't met anyone else who would make me smile and make my heart happy. Thank you, whoever is responsible for that, for giving me the strength to keep that door closed, and for showing me that good men really do exist.

Sleeping Beauty

I remember being madly in love with a man, who once he put his arms around me, I would fall asleep instantly. He used to envy me for how quickly I could fall asleep.

I remember nights of sleeplessness, tossing and turning, lying with my eyes wide open, like golf balls, wondering what in the world I was thinking, wondering why in the world I was choosing to be in a bed with a person who didn't feel the way I did.

I remember my first real moment of love. I remember his arms around me, the room dark, the feeling of security and peace that I felt instantly when he put his arms around me. There was no doubt that I was meant to be there, to be in that moment, and to be rewarded with a good nights sleep. I think the way you sleep when you spend the night with someone is an indicator of how you feel with that person, how you "jive", how you intertwine, how you mix, and if you are meant to be together.

We often turn our eyes and ears to the warning signs. We lie in bed countless nights, wishing the person beside us would hold us, would love us, would cuddle us and keep us warm. We wish they would roll over and hold us and look into our eyes and tell us that they love us and open up their hearts to us. But the truth is, some of them don't.

This is my point. I believe that a compatible relationship is based on many things. The ability to sleep together, no strings attached, just for the sake of holding each other, is purely an indicator of how compatible you are. If you lie awake all night, tossing and turning, thinking you should go home, worrying about everything you have to do tomorrow, wishing you were in your own bed, then it's not meant to be.

Sleep like a baby. Sleep like a princess. Sleep like an angel. And wake up in the arms of someone who thinks you are wonderful, no matter what you look like, if you snore, or how you look in the morning. Find someone who makes you feel warm and safe, and someone who will roll over beside you and be ready to listen to whatever it is you have to say.

Spidey-Senses

It's interesting. I think we all have a gut instinct, but not all of us trust it. It's there for a reason, to guide us, to keep us safe, and to give us insight into what lies ahead of us and the dangers that may be waiting.

I loved the guy. He did everything right. He loved me, or so I thought, and he also hurt me very much. I remember the first time I had a bad feeling, an instinct, that gut feeling that he wasn't being honest with me. I trusted my gut feeling this time, and it was there for a reason.

My girlfriends and I had made plans to head out on the town that night. I had a weird feeling that day in our texts that he was being different, distant, and short with me, and that was not at all who he was, or at least in the ways that I knew him.

I remember him saying he was at a hockey game when I called him, and I had a bad feeling that things weren't right. He never said who he was at the game with, nor did he say which game, but I knew in my heart that he never went to hockey games. Actually, I don't think he even liked the sport. I knew right then, he was not being honest with me, but it would take time before I saw what the future was going to look like.

We cruised the downtown streets together that night, me and the girls. We laughed and giggled, as we passed all of the local bars, trying to pick one out, looking inside to see the crowd.

We were all technically single and hopeful, and perhaps on a bit of a shopping spree that night.

It was as though there was a little monster on my shoulder that night. He knew exactly what I needed to do, and exactly where I needed to be. He kept directing me to go inside this one bar, although we passed many lounges and bars that would have suited us just fine. I couldn't budge the monster, so I forced my friends to go inside, to the local pub that we had all been to before, to find out exactly what was waiting for us and what we were supposed to see.

Once inside and seated, I looked across the room and there it was, the horror, the nightmare, the pain, and the dishonesty that I needed to see. It was the man I was seeing, sitting at the table across from us with a girl, so very clearly on a date with her. Before I could think about what I was doing, I found myself standing in front of their table introducing myself, as I rubbed his back to make sure she knew who I was and that I was a part of his life.

As I walked back to my table, my heart kept telling me the truth. He was on a date, he was cheating on me, and he was lying to me all this time. My head was telling me that maybe he was friends with her, that I shouldn't jump to conclusions so quickly, that I was being stupid. I had sarcastically invited them to join us for a drink before they left, but they quickly drank theirs drinks and walked by our table. Before I could get to the bathroom fast enough, I burst into tears. I knew my heart was right. I just didn't want to believe it.

I spent the next few hours frantically sobbing in the car with the girls, trying to sort out what I had seen. I also spent at least an hour trying to call him, but each time he would hang up when he answered, and I would relentlessly call him back. I knew what he was doing, but I wanted so desperately to hear it from his own mouth.

It wasn't until the next morning, and a night without sleep, that I got the answer that I needed. He finally picked up the phone and told me that he had "picked her", that he met her on vacation, and that I wasn't the one who he wanted. I remember sitting down in the snow and crying harder than a baby. My heart was broken, but the truth needed to be told.

So ladies, please take this with you. We are women. We are smart. We are beautiful. And we are intuitive. Trust your heart and your gut when it is trying to tell you something. If you think something is wrong you need to ask if there is. If you need someone to be honest you need to ask them the right questions. I think sometimes we don't ask things that we perhaps don't want to hear the answers to, but we need to hear these things in order to move forward and to grow.

Don't ever cheat yourself. You deserve great things and kindness. You deserve a man who loves you dearly and a man, who if he knew in his heart that he wasn't in the journey or on the same page as you are, will have the heart to tell you the truth. You deserve that. Don't ever let yourself settle for less because you are worth it.

Xo, Tennessee.

Priests and Sugardaddies

I like to be silly, that's a simple fact about me. When I am with my nearest and dearest of friends and family, I like to laugh and giggle. I have thought for many hours about who would make the perfect man for me, what he would look like, how he would act, and how my family would like him when I brought him home on Christmas Eve.

One day at work, I giggled with my coworkers, as Jenny was talking about her work with the church. I asked, because I have also wondered and been confused, about what type of clergy could marry. She told me that a priest could marry, but only one within the Ukrainian Catholic religion.

I joked with them about this. How funny would it be to marry a priest? He would be kind and beautiful, and have a soul that could reach right into yours. He would have a spirit unlike most, and would be the kind of man who could spend hours sitting and listening to every word that I had to say.

I also giggled about sugar daddies. I have actually thought on more than one occasion, that perhaps it would be worth it to find one. The fact that I am now in my forties, however, does pose a bit of a challenge. Sugar daddies want someone younger, hotter, spicier, perhaps more daring. But nevertheless, I have felt the urge to find one on at least more than one occasion.

"What would a sugar daddy be like?", I thought to myself. Would he be rich and able to buy me the car, the house and the life, that I perhaps could not afford myself? Could he pay off all of my debts and buy me lavish dinners? And would he love me the way that I needed, or tend to my emotional and spiritual needs? I doubt it. Perhaps he would when he was with me, but he would have other girls to tend to once he left my company.

I then thought seriously about this after a few moments of giggles. I don't want a sugar daddy. I don't want to marry a priest. I want to marry a man who loves me for who I am and, regardless of their income or status, is able to communicate with me and care for me the way that I want him to.

Me and Eric

Let's face it, dating these days is tough, extremely tough, and not for the lighthearted. We are troopers trying to stay on board, and figure out what the hell is going on. We will get our hearts broken, probably a few times before we meet a real prince, but we have to keep trying. Nobody said it was going to be easy.

It's funny. Everytime I have invested in someone, only to find they have now moved on, or got back together with their ex-wife, I tell myself that I will be okay. Sometimes I cry, others I laugh. But each and every time I wipe my tears, put on my runners, and keep going. I listen to Eric Church, my hero, and tell myself it's going to be okay.

You will find him, so just take a deep breath. Have a hot bath. Be good to yourself. Being hard on yourself only hurts you. You are wonderful. He didn't deserve you. And I promise someone will someday deserve you, and until then be proud of you, and be okay with being single.

Spend time with, and on, you. Be good to you. Be proud of who you are. This life is a beautiful one, and you must remember to count all of your blessings, albeit a cat who loves you dearly, a friend who makes you laugh, a co-worker who makes each work day better, or a mom who always loves you back. Never ever lose hope.

Do You Hear What I Hear?

Sometimes we need to put down our phones, stop filling in the blanks and be honest with ourselves.

If a guy's texts are random, they probably aren't investing in you. If they're late night or drunk texts, maybe they only think about you when they're drunk. If they only send you emoticons, they probably have nothing to say. It's like Morse code. You need to be smart to decipher the code. Some guys aren't good communicators. Some guys aren't good people. Some will tell you what they think you want to hear, until it's too hard for them to fake it anymore. The texts get shorter. The responses take longer. They just "disappear".

Let's be honest. Put down your damn phone and enjoy that very moment in reality. If you met a guy who walked up to you and said hello, and then told you he liked you and wanted to get to know you, that you're beautiful and smart and sweet, and then a few minutes later walked away from your table and never came back, would you sit there and wait for him until he did? No girl, you wouldn't, so stop waiting.

If you went on a date and all a guy did was sit and make faces at you, stuck out his tongue or blushed the whole time and said nothing, would you think he's cool and that he liked you? I doubt it, and you would probably think he's messed up and weird. It's hard to read into a whole bunch of words that may sometimes mean nothing.

If you were on a date and you asked a guy a question and it took him three days to answer, would you wait? I doubt that you would. Texting sucks, let's face it. My computer doesn't make me happy. It doesn't make me feel special, It can't talk to me. But I can sit there on it for hours and daydream, and think about anything I want to.

So what does a smart girl do? Trust your instinct. Don't read into texts. A guy who truly cares about you makes an effort. He will take you on dates, buy you dinner, and be proud and ready to show you off to the real world.

All The Same

You know I often question if I will remarry or if I will find the love of my life, or if I am simply destined to be single for the rest of my life. Then I tell myself who really cares? Life happens the way it's supposed to, and I don't think worrying about it is going to change that.

Man or woman, I think we all want the same things. We want to be touched. We want to be loved. And we want to bring joy into others lives and reciprocally, we want them to bring joy to ours.

To every man I have met on this journey I have been living, thank you. You have each taught me a valuable life lesson, whether it be about you, or about myself, all in all it's been a lesson.

So ladies, I don't know if I am any wiser since this dating journey began, but I am stronger and more beautiful in my heart. You are beautiful too, just by knowing and appreciating your own strengths and weaknesses and your own self worth.

Don't ever stop believing in something bigger than yourself, or lose faith that you are on the right path. Life takes us in many directions, and I think each one of those directions is right for us in its own way.

Look for the one who makes you feel like they cannot live without you. Or, as my dear friend put it, find the one who says "I'm looking for that connection I can't be without. The person that I think of as soon as I wake every morning. That person I can't truly be myself with, without fear of being judged" and make that person they are looking for - you.

Love. Listen. Care. Cherish. Appreciate. They are all of the things that matter. You are on the right path and when that person is meant to be, they will drop down in front of you and you won't help but run into them. Never give up. Love with all you've got. Xo, TJ.

Like It, Love It, Or Leave It

Well it's simple. You can take me as I am, like me as I am, or leave me as I am and walk away.

I truly believe all women have wonderful qualities. Most of us don't see them or know they are there, but everyone around us knows they are there. Sometimes we each need to be reminded that we are wonderful, beautiful, smart, funny, kind, caring, witty, responsible, sweet, wonderful and just that we are good people. Everyone needs that. So don't you dare settle for someone who forgets to notice who you really are.

I remember dating someone who didn't always have the same beliefs that I did. I tried to be what he wanted me to be, and forgot who I really was, and truly I wasn't happy. I tried to pretend I didn't like to have an occasional beer, or that I didn't like to play VLTs, but deep down I was only lying to myself. I couldn't hide who I was, nor did I really want to, and one can only pretend to be something they are not for a short time. I don't regret what I did, or the time I spent with him. But I do regret not being able to stand my ground, fight for what I believe in, and for defending my choices. I am proud to say that I have grown and am now fully confident in telling someone what I believe, how I feel, and what is important to me.

We all have a purpose. We are meant to be here for a reason. We are here to do something wonderful, and something that makes a difference. We need to be in relationships that recognize that. We cannot forget our good qualities and our blessings, and we need to be appreciated every day for who we are. We need to wake up every day, and if we are in a relationship, be reminded verbally or just in spirit that we are good.

So when that person stomps into the front door and thinks they can walk all over you and your good heart, remember to shut the door quickly and run as fast as you can. They don't deserve you. You deserve better. And remember if they don't like you as you are, they can like you, love you or leave you. If they chose to leave, you are better off. Save your greatness for someone else who will appreciate who you are and what you have to offer.

Xo

Meant To Be

I'm not really sure this chapter is about dating, but it's about life and I feel it needs to be part of my book.

Life is never easy. Some days we laugh, some days we struggle, some days we see the light at the end of the tunnel. But each and every day that we get the chance to live, to breathe, to love, to feel the joy of this crazy thing we call life, we really are blessed. There are so many things I find myself grateful for, and I wanted to share this story with you.

It was a recent diagnosis for my very dear friend with cancer. She is beautiful and kind, and each moment I spend with her is one filled with laughter, joy and love. She has given much of her life to helping others and her fight with cancer has been tough, but she and I have been trying to fight it together, one moment, one giggle, and one day at a time.

I came across an opportunity to see a well-known heavy metal band in our local city. It was crazy and happened by chance, after making friends with someone who got me two free tickets and VIP passes to the show. I was ecstatic. I knew exactly who needed to join me that night.

She and I arrived at the show. We quickly raced to the counter to pick up our tickets and opened the tightly sealed envelope. Inside were two nearly front row seats, and two VIP passes to the friends and family room. We quickly raced up the elevator and through the crowd, like two teenagers going to their first Springsteen concert, to find the room.

We walked in and felt a bit nervous, looking around to see who the other guests were, glowing with the feeling of being special for that moment and night. As I texted our new friend he quickly came to get us, walking us down to the stage to see the rest of what the music world is all about. It was amazing; my heart was almost bursting with excitement and ready to jump right out of my chest, and yet I was almost frozen in time in awe of what was happening.

We walked along the bottom of the stage, while men and women stared in awe at us, wondering how we were so lucky to be there, mingling among the outskirts, where only the band would be walking, feeling at that moment like rock stars ourselves. As he walked us up to an area where many guitars were leaned up against the stage waiting to be played, we had no idea what was about to happen.

As he placed a guitar carefully around each of our necks, we blushed and panicked, worried that we were doing something illegal, something crazy, something the rest of the world never gets to do. Here I was, in the middle of one of the most talented bands in the world, holding the band member's guitars. We both stood still in amazement. We asked ourselves if this could really be happening.

We quickly walked to our seats and realized we were close enough to the stage to see the look on each member's face, the style of their clothing, the brand of their shoes, and the glory of what they must feel like to be a star. I cannot say I have rocked that hard at a concert before, ever really in my life, or felt the chill up my spine like I did that very moment and place in time that night. After the show, I couldn't sleep. We were given guitar picks that we held in our hands like teenagers. We also received the original set list that the band played that night.

I guess my glory in that moment was this. The Gentleman, for I cannot properly describe him any other way, treated us with kindness and respect, and gave us his full heart and passion for music for each and every one of the moments that we spent with him. He made two small town girls lives sparkle in that moment. He touched us in so many ways with his kindness, I cannot be anything else but grateful and to feel blessed.

To the man who made this all happen, all I can say is thank you. I told you in that moment how grateful we really were, but I think it deserves to be written down in this book, because you restored my faith in both mankind, the gift of giving, and in the feeling of being blessed. Thank you for sharing your world and heart with us.

I woke up the next morning, not because I had to, but because I wanted to. I hadn't felt that joy and passion for life in a long time and couldn't be more grateful. I realized again in that moment that every single day is truly a gift. We can choose to pretend there are no gifts in each day, or we can chose to see them and acknowledge them and remind ourselves why we are here. Every day we have a reason, a purpose and many gifts, and we need to wake each day believing in goodness. Some things in life will never be easy. Others are simply meant to be.

The End

Little did they realize that they would only be a page or a piece of a chapter in a silly little book about dating. All of the men who lied their way into my lives or mislead me into believing they were in it for the right reasons, well thank you. You have helped me on my journey, helped me to learn what I want and need in my life, and helped me to heal.

And, to the beautiful, loving, kind gentlemen that I have met, I also express a heartfelt thank you. You have brought joy into my life, even if you were only passing through it, and touched me in more ways than I can probably express. As I look back I realize it was all meant to be. I was meant to meet each and every one of you, just as you are, so that I could share these stories with you.

I guess each time I thought that I had met the one, I realized that the "one" was still out there waiting for me. Each time my heart broke, I would pick up my sad little heart and take a deep breath and try it again. I tried not to lose hope, and in the end I realize that I didn't.

The more I think about it, the more I realize that people are all looking for the same things. They want to be loved. They want to be appreciated. They want to share their lives with someone. For some, however, they only want to share pieces of their lives or pieces of their hearts, and for others, they are ready and willing to dive right in and give all of their heart to you.

I remember a quote in the movie "Premonition", with Sandra Bullock, that never left my mind. I write about hope, like they talked about it in the movie, when Sandra goes to see a priest in her church. The priest tells her that some things in life are not seen by the eye, but they are felt by the heart, like hope and love. I really believe that we have to appreciate that gift. Hope and love are felt by the heart. They are free. No one has the power to take away what your heart feels, or the hope that you have, and you need to remember that. They are true gifts that we need to honor and take advantage of.

My point is simple. I never lost hope on my quest to find true love. I never lost hope, and the faith that by the time I finished writing this book, that I would have found my knight in shining armor, my Prince, my soulmate. Truth be known, I did find him. He is kind, thoughtful and sweet, and he adores me for exactly who I am. I get excited every time I see him, or his words light up my phone, and I am truly thankful that our lives crossed paths.

I also know there is someone for everyone. Our task is to find them. Don't give up. Have faith that they are out there looking for you. You will find them or they will find you. And remember, regardless of how much pressure both we and society put on ourselves to find that person, the only person who can love you more than anybody is you.

Love yourself like crazy. Be proud of everything that you are and that you believe in. Believe in the goodness in people, and believe that you have exactly what the perfect person for you will be looking for. Don't lose hope. Be patient. Love is beautiful and we are all searching for it. I just know that you will find him. In the meantime, put on your runners, hop on that bike, and take every chance you get to enjoy every blessing, in every minute, in this big old adventure we call life. All my Love, Tennessee.

Acknowledgements

Amritraj, A., Jashni, J., Shankman, A., Gibgot, J., Perkash, S., Hamson, N. (Producers), & Yapo, M. (Director). (2007). Premonition (motion picture). USA: Tristar Pictures.

Bud Light, MD Anheuser-Busch, LLC. One Busch Place, St. Louise, MO, 63118.

Eharmony.com, 2000, web address accessed April 2, 2018, http://www.en.m.wikipedia.org .

Eric Church, Singer-songwriter, Nashville, TN, USA.

Goldberg, D., Phillips, T. (Producers), & Phillips, T. (Director). (2009). The Hangover (motion picture). USA: Warner Brothers Pictures.

Harrah's Las Vegas Hotel and Casino, Las Vegas, NV, USA.

Gottlieb, L. (Producer), & Ardolina, E. (Director). (1987). Dirty Dancing (motion picture), USA: Vestron Pictures.

John R. Cash, Singer-songwriter, Nashville, TN, USA.

Juvonen, N., Disco, M., Stronan, G. (Producers), & Kwapis, K. (Director). (2009). He's Just Not that into You (motion picture). USA: Flower Films.

Margaritaville Restaurant, Las Vegas, NV, USA.

Martina, T. (Director). 2016. Zombie Burlesque. Planet Hollywood Resort, Las Vegas, NV, USA.

Match.com, 1995, web address accessed April 2, 2018, http://www.en.m.wikipedia.org .

POF.com, Plenty of Fish Media, 2003, web address accessed April 2, 2018, http://www.en.m.wikipedia.org .

Presley, E. (1964). Viva Las Vegas. "Viva Las Vegas". Retrieved from http://www.en.m.wikipedia.org .

Shania Twain, Singer-songwriter, Timmins, Ontario, CAN.

Victoria's Secret Stores LLC, 2 Limited Pkwy, Columbus, Ohio, USA, 43230.

Walt Disney (Producer), & Geronimi, C., Larson, E., Reitherman, W., Clark, L. (Directors). (1959). Sleeping Beauty (motion picture). USA: Walt Disney Productions.

Made in the USA
Lexington, KY
05 April 2019